P9-BAU-287

The Practitioner Inquiry Series

Marilyn Cochran-Smith and Susan L. Lytle, *SERIES EDITORS*

ADVISORY BOARD: Rebecca Barr, Judy Buchanan, Robert Fecho,
Susan Florio-Ruane, Sarah Freedman, Karen Gallas, Andrew Gitlin,
Dixie Goswami, Peter Grimmett, Gloria Ladson-Billings, Roberta Logan,
Sarah Michaels, Susan Noffke, Marsha Pincus, Marty Rutherford,
Lynne Strieb, Carol Tateishi, Polly Ulichny, Diane Waff, Ken Zeichner

"Sometimes I Can Be Anything":
Power, Gender, and Identity
in a Primary Classroom
KAREN GALLAS

Learning in Small Moments:
Life in an Urban Classroom
DANIEL R. MEIER

Interpreting Teacher Practice:
Two Continuing Stories
RENATE SCHULZ

Creating Democratic Classrooms:
The Struggle to Integrate Theory and Practice
LANDON E. BEYER, Editor

"Sometimes I Can Be Anything"

Power, Gender, and Identity in a Primary Classroom

KAREN GALLAS

TEACHERS COLLEGE PRESS

Teachers College, Columbia University
New York and London

Published by Teachers College Press, 1234 Amsterdam Avenue, New York, NY 10027

Library of Congress Cataloging-in-Publication Data

Gallas, Karen.
    Sometimes I can be anything : power, gender, and identity in a
primary classroom / Karen Gallas.
        p.   cm. — (The practitioner inquiry series)
    Includes bibliographical references (p.   ) and index.
    ISBN 0-8077-3696-1 (cloth). — ISBN 0-8077-3695-3 (pbk.)
    1. Sex differences in education—United States—Case studies.
2. Education, Primary—Social aspects—United States—Case studies.
3. Gender identity—United States—Case studies.   4. Interaction
analysis in education—United States—Case studies.   I. Title.
II. Series.
LC212.92.G35   1998
372.24'1—dc21   97-36157

ISBN 0-8077-3695-3 (paper)
ISBN 0-8077-3696-1 (cloth)

Printed on acid-free paper
Manufactured in the United States of America

05   04   8   7   6   5   4   3

For the Children of 1–2 G

Contents

Acknowledgments

This was a very difficult book to write. In fact, even from the beginning of data collection, it was hard for me to articulate what I thought was going on. However, my colleagues in the Brookline Teacher Research Seminar were very generous with their thoughts and their time and helped me get on my way.

Because being a teacher researcher is really two jobs, by the time I was ready to begin tackling the writing of this book, I was very tired. My husband, Dave Edwards, strongly suggested that I take a year off from teaching to work *only* on this manuscript. Then he very generously supported me, both materially and psychically, as I struggled with the writing.

Two years later I had finally finished the manuscript, or so I thought. At that point my colleague Ann Phillips gave it a careful reading, and her notes helped me to be clearer in many parts. Following that, my editor at Teachers College Press, Carol Chambers Collins, began to scrutinize the text. Her critique, and her desire for clarity about a difficult subject, sent me back to write some more and enabled me to *really* finish the manuscript.

To all these people, my deepest thanks.

My comprehension of the world, my dreams of the world, my judgment of the world—all of these are part of my individual practice; all speak of my presence in the world. I need all of this to begin to understand myself. But it is not sufficient to explicate my actions. In the final analysis, consciousness is socially bred.

—*Paolo Freire (1987)*

Gender as Performance

Field Notes: February

The bad boys are in the block corner. They are playing alien Klingons, all in their stocking feet . . . they are all talking at once.

TONY: Mega Tornado going through. Let's send out the space ants.
CHARLES: I'll send them out. (He gently tosses a few toy cars out of the structure.)
MICHAEL (throwing a few more cars out): Space ants are out.
TONY: Space helicopters ready. They're flying (helicopter noises). They're letting out ants. (More cars fly out.)
CHARLES (In a high, baby voice): Daddy! Lookit, Daddy, lookit, space ants!

> *'Can I sit with Patchy again?' asks Matawhero.*
> *I look at him from my low chair in perplexity. This question has a significance of some kind if only I could put my finger on it . . . really, it's confusing, this overlapping of two worlds. Does it amount to a fall or a rise, this crossing through the trees?*
> *'Can I?'*
> *'I beg your pardon?' I brush my face again more severely as though there were cobwebs collected upon it, obscuring my view. And to an extent it works, because whereas before I felt there was some significance in this thought of Matawhero's, now I realize there is even more to it. If only I could see what's under my nose. I take a deep breath and concentrate. 'What did you say, Matawhero?'*
>
> *—Ashton-Warner, (1958)*

When I entered the classroom as a novice teacher more than twenty years ago, I was sure that my work would create new worlds of possibility for children. Day after day and year after year I returned to that work, taking

1

the promise of possibility more and more for granted, and finding the real world of children to be my anchor. On a mundane, everyday level, I just wanted to teach well. But as the years progressed, my concept of "teaching well" altered and good teaching became more than believing that I was covering important curricula and that children were mastering subject matter. The social and political began to loom large as driving concerns. Children's desires for affiliation, their need to play and create new worlds, pressed in. Issues of power and entitlement, of alienation and failure, of silent or silenced complicated the process. They crowded me as I worked, pushing my focus on content aside, causing me to doubt myself and to want to give the children more space to position themselves in the world, to work through those problems that might hobble them in their own lives, to create their own worlds of possibility.

I wondered what was the most important part of my work. Was it to get the content across, or to get out of the way of the very serious work that children do below the surface? Or were those concerns inseparable? The classroom became a laboratory for life as I perceived that what children studied and needed to know was decidedly more than the subject areas I had been hired to teach.

GENDER AND EQUITY

For the past 20 years, researchers and others have asserted that the pursuit of sex equity in education is a critical component of realizing gender equality in the adult world, and that that pursuit must be negotiated in the day-to-day dynamics of the classroom. An AAUW report (1993) has repeated the call for educators to reexamine their approaches to curriculum and classroom management, and document their observations and outcomes. I was trained in the 1970s, during the first flush of the sex equity movement, and embraced that objective as part of my work to create new worlds of possibility for children. Like many teachers, I struggled each day to help children diversify their understandings of gender and race and class.

I now believe, however, after spending four years inspecting the boundaries and the interiors of gender relations in my classroom, that the construction of a "gender-balanced classroom" is a goal that reflects incomplete understandings of classroom life and denies the dynamic cultural milieu of today's classrooms. Sex equity—and, in fact, all efforts to understand and remedy inequity and social bias—need to be redefined based on a different framework of how classroom life evolves over time. When it is reported that "research spanning the past 20 years consistently reveals that males receive more teacher attention than do females" (AAUW, p. 60), all teachers agree. We know that "boys demand more attention" (p. 68), that "appropriate behaviors for boys include . . . exerting power over girls—or other, weaker boys" (p. 73). We know these things as part of the reality of classroom life. What we do not always know is how these circumstances come about: the conditions within which social relations become codified as reality in a particular classroom.

As Barrie Thorne points out, "children's collective activities should weigh more fully in our overall understanding of gender and social life" (1993, p. 4). Descriptions that take into account the important roles of language, culture, and classroom discourse can assist us as we attempt to negotiate the uneven and changeable terrain that often defines the social climate of the classroom, a climate heavily influenced by children's (and teachers') understandings of social discourse. Proactive methods of instruction, consciousness raising, and gender-neutral or multi-cultural materials are *tools* that can help teachers teach better. However, classrooms are more than rooms full of children waiting to be taught. They are dialogic communities (Bakhtin, 1986), where understandings of texts and social relations are collectively forged, with and without the teacher's knowledge and assistance.

PURPOSE

Pedagogical practice represents a particular politics of experience that is a cultural field where knowledge, discourse, and power intersect so as to produce historically specific practices of moral and social regulation. . . . This problematic points to the need to interrogate how human experiences are produced, contested, and legitimated within the dynamics of everyday classroom life.
                                                            —*Giroux (1985, p. 23)*

In this book I hope to provide the reader with an in-depth look at how the children I taught worked to understand the social terrain of the classroom and how I as their teacher made sense of their work. The research in this book began as an attempt to provide a description of how children "do gender" (West & Zimmerman, 1987). My intention was to add to other accounts that focus on the construction of gender in elementary settings (Best, 1983; Paley, 1984; Thorne, 1993). Over time, however, it became clear that the children I taught did not naturally separate their understandings of gender from those of race or class. They did not categorize their social actions according to a particular kind of stratification, much as I and other adults might. Their interactions were much more socially holistic—that is, they were rooted in the contexts of their particular historicial moment in school, and it became clear to me that much of what I saw had to do with issues of power and social control.

Anne Dyson (1993) calls the work children do to bring their lives into the mainstream of classroom social life the building of "classroom neighborhoods." In my opinion, the dynamics of how these neighborhoods are built revolve around subtle manipulations of personal and collective power. I saw that children used different kinds of performances to mediate what Edwards and Mercer have called the "power asymmetry" of the classroom (1987, p. 158). They described that asymmetry as resulting from the teacher's natural authority in the classroom. However, based on my belief that the teacher is not the sole actor in the drama of classroom life, I would like to extend their metaphor to include children, looking closely at the natural authority or lack of it that children bring to the classroom as an extension of their home culture, and consider the ways in which all children attempt to negotiate power relationships within a classroom community.

I have learned that the intensity of children's efforts in this process creates a *subtextual dynamic* that permeates both the social and academic domains of schooling. (See Chapter 1 for a description of the subtextual.) In looking at the children's work over time, I have come to see that their desire to be part of a classroom community has a powerful influence on their work with *every* kind of classroom text, both those they created, and those I presented to them. Offered here is a description of how these kinds of dynamics unfold, and also of how my work as a teacher researcher changed the way I viewed both my role and the children's in shaping social discourse. In essence, this book attempts to "interrogate" how the dynamics I witnessed and participated in were, as Henry Giroux wrote, "produced, contested, and legimated" over time.

RESEARCH PERSPECTIVE

La frontera is a place where cultures can collide creatively such that the identities of those who "cross over" are enriched and challenged. Identities that are not simply vehicles for the production of sameness, for the reproduction of racial authenticity and purity, but identities that can enable us to cross borders and experience different cultural locations. We lack an adequate language to talk about race or theorize subjectivity and identity and their relationship to cultural determination, one that escapes the binarisms of the dominant discourse of male vs. female, rich vs. poor, white vs. black.
                                          —*Estrada & McClaren (1993, pp. 28-29)*

Developing a clear research perspective has become, by necessity, a second purpose of this book. My research has evolved through several stages and different perspectives, but it initially began with a teacher's orientation: I wanted to understand how particular children, specifically bad boys and silent girls, influenced classroom dynamics so that I could have more control over those dynamics. At that point I thought I was undertaking a general observation of the social relations among 6-, 7-, and 8-year-old children from the perspective of their different genders.

However, as I began to write about these relations, I realized that the kinds of events I had witnessed and interpreted as gender-specific behaviors in fact were not so easily categorized. When I reviewed my data and tried to describe different incidents, my understanding of the purposes and motives behind the children's interactions grew muddier over time. Writing became a painful process: the children I had loved and observed so closely suddenly became symbols of every social problem that I personally found troubling. I was unable to separate what I had observed and recorded in the classroom from my own social viewpoints and events in the society at large. Sexism, racism, sexual harassment, victimization of the less able—it seemed to me that the children in my little microcosm were simply in training to be adults in a society divided by race, culture, language, religion, and economics.

In struggling to understand my data, I couldn't seem to sort out the nature of the children's conflicts. Were they about the differences between boys and girls, or the differences between children within and across the sexes? Were they about power, or friendship? Did they reflect different social abilities, or the heirarchies of race and class? Finally, after several confused months, I was able to adopt a point of view that enabled me to think about what I had observed outside of my own limitations as an adult member of American society in the last decade of this century. I saw that the children experienced the classroom as "la frontera", territory to be mapped.

As I examined the children's active attempts to make their world sensible and reliable, and the resulting stances they assumed to maintain that sensibility, I saw that I had to push aside my own personal labels for the behavior I was seeing. For example, *for children* the concept of "sexism" or "sexist" is not a known one until that label is defined and applied by an adult; the state of being "silenced" can originate in an active assumption of "silence" as a desirable position within the social milieu; the act of harassment begins with overtures of friendship; what I perceive as racism is often a form of retaliation against an impersonal and vulnerable target. Without labels I became more able to see how what I now call *social breaches or ruptures* begin. Children's interactions do not come loaded with the political and psychosocial metaphors of the adult world. Thus their conflicts and dilemmas in many ways are timeless and constantly shifting. We can see through them how tensions and miscommunications arise, how and why power is coveted and used to control others, and the points at which resolutions are possible.

Performance as a Framework

> *Gender boundaries have a shifting presence, but when evoked they are accompanied by stylized forms of action, a sense of performance, mixed and ambiguous meanings.*
>
> —*Thorne (1993)*

To maintain an attitude of openness to the data, I reconceptualized the children's ongoing social interactions as a series of performances that were continually reinvented on a daily basis. This insight came to me when I began working on the concept of "posing" (see Chapter 5), because the children I had observed were so clearly in a performance mode. As I worked with other kinds of data, I saw that over time the children's performances required them to assume and work inside the body of many different characters. I began to think of these characters as different *personae*. Some of the children would experiment with different characters from day to day, while others would become entrenched in more serious and long-term personae that often locked them into difficult social dynamics.

This approach to viewing children's social interactions as dramatic encounters encompasses both the notion of performance as fictional in nature and performance as representing the development of a public self. It is both an imaginative act and a representation of what is real in the child's life, and it includes an acute awareness of audience. Often this public character provides a direct contrast to the child's private or personal self. Thus I saw children as both in and outside their bodies, perceiving different realities in the world around them, identifying different roles that were open to them, and experimenting in the social milieu of the school with those roles that attracted them and seemed to "fit" within their present world.

I do not see these performances as subliminal; neither do I see them as completely within the child's control. They were usually not scripted, although in some cases a few children clearly had planned an event to see what effect it would have. Therefore the work they did to figure out their social world can best be characterized as improvisations on a theme. As with any improvisation, the chain of events, though not necessarily within the performers' control, is not initiated in an unthinking way. Further, in an improvisation, the audience, in subtle ways, guides and shapes the performance. Thus every child in the class is a "player," even if she or he is simply an onlooker. Children in their daily interactions are active intelligences, studying the social exchanges that surround them, evaluating the meanings behind those exchanges, and then modifying, reconceptualizing, and/or confirming their own social strategies within the context of their relationships.

If we consider the tremendous amount of information, both concrete and subliminal, that children encounter on a daily basis, and the ways in which much of that information is contradictory and sometimes antagonistic, their attempts to sort out that morass through the medium of performance and play become much more powerful as representations of their world. Friends, parents, teachers, neighbors, siblings, extended family, adults they encounter in their community—and finally, within a more nebulous and intangible world, their semiotic contacts with mass culture: television, movies, videos, music, books, magazines, newpapers, and radio—each of these presses in, demanding attention and dispensing information and opinions. It is no wonder that children play with such intensity and creative skill and that their improvisations within the protected world of school are pursued with passion and sincerity. Their world and the expectations of society are confusing and complex. Only within the context of play and imaginative reenactments of their world can they develop and test their constantly evolving interpretations of what is and is not possible for them as social actors.

GENDER AS A STARTING POINT

I now believe that while many of the social experiments in my classroom began with gender-specific behaviors, their outcomes often took them into other realms which were not always linked in adult minds with gender or sexuality. Just as children do not learn to read or write in isolation from their efforts to become part of a community (Ashton-Warner, 1963; Atwell, 1986; Dyson, 1993; Heath, 1983, among others) so they do not experiment with social relations in discrete categories. In a classroom where the creation of a close community is a goal and structures are put into place to encourage that goal, the boundaries between gender, race, and class become quite fuzzy over time. Stereotypes about sex-typed behavior are also called into question when we consider the contexts in which they occur. For example, both boys and girls use language to exclude others, but boys use a public forum for that language while girls employ the private realm. That specific difference in language use results in completely different social effects in the classroom: one is a strategy used quite pointedly in public discourse and often has far greater effect on classroom climate, while the other is carried out as a more sequestered activity and produces effects more subtle and personal. The descriptions in this book peel back the outer layer of gender and show the guts, as it were, of children's social relations.

THE CHILDREN

The children in this book (with the exception of those in the afterword) represent two classes of first- and second-grade children I taught for two years each, over a four-year period. The children in the afterword were first graders who I taught for one year following the completion of the rough draft of this book. All the children were from predominantly middle- and upper-middle-class professional families, with approximately 20 percent from working class homes. As a rule my classes are diverse, both culturally and linguistically, and include Asians, African Americans, and Latinos, while approximately one-half are Caucasian. Many of the children are new immigrants from China, Southeast Asia, and Japan, although some of my students are newly arrived from Africa and the Middle East.

Some of the children in this book are initially represented by me from a stereotypic viewpoint, and that is because in watching them I could not avoid naming the characters or personae they had adopted and maintained throughout the two years I observed them. For example, the reader will meet the "bad boys," Tony and Tom, who enter this book as second graders, and Andrew, Michael, and Charles, who followed enthusiastically in their footsteps a year later; Josie, a "tom boy"; "beautiful" Dierdre; Latia and Alexis, "proud and taking no risks"; and Rachel, a "silent girl." Other children are important figures in different events throughout the book, although they defy neat catergorizations because of the flexibility and earnestness of their efforts: Germaine, who entered my class as a second grader and worked hard to belong; Ellen and Mia, both inquisitive and egalitarian in their approach to community and comfortable taking risks in the public domain; Donald, close friend of the bad boys with a good boy's style. Because I describe only those events that took place in public, some children will be seen only briefly in this book. They were individuals who, although less visible, were still active participants in the daily transactions of the classroom. Pseudonyms are used for all the children.

THE CLASSROOM

My classroom is part of an urban, K–8 elementary school in what might be characterized as a school system with a progressive history of instruction, a reputation for academic excellence, and a commitment to serving the needs of all children. Because the school system is quite diverse, teachers are encouraged to provide their students with ongoing exposure to the cultures and traditions of all our students. We use literature and resources and plan classroom activities and special events that honor the artistic, social, and literary traditions of many cultures. Further, teachers are encouraged to reflect upon the ways that issues of race, class, and gender affect their instruction and children's success in school.

Many of the texts and events reported here were observed and audiotaped in particular classroom times that occur regularly each week and are deliberately planned to encourage children to talk together without my direct orchestration. I refer to sharing time, science talks, morning journal times: these periods are linked by their emphasis on child-directed interactions, and they originated from my interest as a teacher researcher in exploring children's language in both public and private contexts. Sharing time is a daily event when the children have an opportunity to sit in the teacher's chair. The sharing child directs his or her own time in the chair while my role in this period is to be a member of the audience. I do not orchestrate the child's presentation or direct the class's responses by choosing who asks questions or makes comments. Some children bring in an object from home; some tell what we call "fake stories," and those are usually completely improvised; some present a "mystery," which is a problem situation the class then tries to solve; some talk about an event in their life; some bring a formal complaint to the class about a part of school life; some distribute food they've cooked, or natural treasures they've found outside. Every child has a designated day on which he or she can share, but no child is forced to do so. It is my experience that eventually all the children participate in sharing. Many of my observations and recorded texts are obtained during sharing time, and as time passes, the children become more completely themselves: their guard is dropped, social conventions are manipulated, and real agendas surface. (For a more in-depth look at sharing time, see Gallas, 1994.)

Science talks take place on a weekly basis and are times when the class, either as a whole or, more rarely, in small groups, discusses a child's (or, less often, a teacher's) question about science. The questions are not closed ones that have only one right answer—for example, "Who was the first person on the moon?" They are big-picture questions open to broad speculation—for example, "Why did the dinosaurs die?" The purpose of the talks is to encourage all the children to talk about science, to think and theorize together, to wonder out loud. Some of the texts cited in this book were obtained during science talks and other similar whole class discussions. (For a further look at science talks, see Gallas, 1995.)

There is a time at the beginning of the day when the children work in their art journals. These volumes include drawings, collages, writings, poems, notes to friends, games, mazes, sketches, and origami. When the children work in their journals they may sit wherever they want and talk quietly with their friends. Often the children ask to share their journals with the whole class during sharing time, which follows the art journal period. I view this time as a way for the children to ease themselves into the school day, and the journals as an important way for the children to develop different kinds of personal expressive skills. Both my observations of the children during the early morning period and the work they do in their journals informs my work as a teacher and a researcher.

Other events in this book were observed on the playground at recess or resulted from formal discussions and interviews that I convened in response to a classroom dilemma. Because the children and I believe that their ideas are important, there were daily opportunities for them to talk together without my active control. Through these I am able to witness what I would term much more "naturalistic" social interactions. In other words, when I actively listen to children as they talk together, but refrain from moderating or commenting on their discussions, the children become more visible, more public, and more articulate over time.

The classroom incidents presented here were selected as examples because they represented clear and compelling examples of events that I had observed over and over again in different classes for several years. When I describe a particular incident, I am doing so because I see the event as symbolic. In other words, when I cite a particular child's actions as a character, or one kind of performance as a scenario, it is because that action repeated itself over time.

STRUCTURE OF THE BOOK

With the exception of Chapters 1 and 11, this book is ordered chronologically. The sequence of chapters is intended to give the reader a sense of how my focus as a researcher changed over time. I often had the image, as I thought about this piece of work, that I was like a beachcomber. At first, taken with the texture, color, and shape of sea glass, the novice beachcomber picks up every piece. It is the aesthetic and physical phenomenon, the action of water on glass over years, the delight in finding treasure strewn over a beach that fascinates, and the collection process is almost indiscriminate. Later, blue glass becomes the prize because it is so rare, and in the process of looking for the blue glass the beachcomber's focus narrows. As it does, the beachcomber begins to notice subtleties of color and shape: how one color of glass can best be seen when it lies close to a contrasting color. Soon the collector widens her search again to consider how blue interacts with other colors and shapes, and as she does she notices new colors, textures, and even materials to be collected.

So it is that the narrative in this book begins, in Chapter 2, with snapshots from what I call the "gender circus." When a teacher begins to look for the presence of gender dynamics in the classroom, they are found, like sea glass on the beach, everywhere. But their meaning and impact, their history and development, their relationship to one another and to the process of teaching and learning, are not clear. My research process narrowed only when I was confronted with a teaching problem that was connected to gender dynamics. In other words, I had to narrow my focus to see the blue glass, as it were, to search it out and hold onto it so that I could bring my classroom back into control. Chapter 3 represents that narrowing of focus and looks closely at bad boys and the ways in which they worked to gain power and hold onto it. Chapter 4 provides an account of my struggle to work with a silent girl who, in ways similar to the bad boys, disrupted my vision of who was powerful in the teaching and learning process.

Chapters 5 through 10 illustrate how my focus broadened again, after a close focus on bad boys and a silent girl, to include more communal issues of gender and the ways it was being socially constructed by *all* the children. In Chapter 5, the notion of "posing" as a way to influence other children is introduced. This chapter represents my first awareness that some children were orchestrating performances for social purposes. Chapter 6 describes the development of what I came to call the Saturday game, a game that was orchestrated by the bad boys to shape classroom discourse for the purposes of play and entertainment.

Chapter 7 uncovers the dynamics of boys and girls trying to make authentic contact as friends after spending two years together. It focuses closely on the ways in which each group communicates at cross purposes. Chapters 8 and 9 continue to consider miscommunication as a source of tension among children and describe how, as the boys in my class struggled for recognition and power, gender dynamics became intertwined with issues of race, culture, status, and belonging. In contrast, Chapter 10 focuses on girls in public and the different paths they took to take control of their identities within the social milieu.

In contrast to the chronological arrangement of Chapters 2 through 10, Chapters 1 and 11 provide synthesizing perspectives. Chapter 1 outlines the evolution of my perspective over the course of the entire research and writing process and gives a detailed look at the concept of the subtextual, which I developed as a way to explain how gender influences the purposes of teachers and children. That chapter represents thinking that developed over 6 years, including 4 years of data collection and 2 of writing to complete the manuscript. Similarly, Chapter 11 looks at the children's actions from the point of view of their imaginal purposes and their aspirations to cross boundaries and experience new worlds of possibility. It returns to my original questions about my role as a teacher and the children's goals as learners.

Finally, I have included an afterword, specifically to bring the reader back to the question of the conditions within which we construct our understandings of social and political realities. This chapter is meant to prod the reader (as I was prodded by a new first-grade class) to consider, within his or her own life, how ideas about gender, race, class, and power must always be called into question. It is, most important, a tribute to the lessons that each new group of children can teach us about what we *must not* assume.

POINT OF VIEW

It is important to reiterate my intention in writing this book, and the kinds of constructs that have helped me to think about this work. My purpose here is to provide the reader with an in-depth look at the children I taught and the ways in which they negotiated issues of power in my classroom. To do that I have developed conceptual frameworks that have helped me to write about them descriptively rather than interpretively. Those frameworks include the idea of *performance* as a way to view children's actions, children's assumption of *personae* as a means to try on different social roles, and *topography* as a way to characterize the social terrain of each classroom community. Further, to understand the implications of the children's actions for their success as learners, I developed the idea of the *subtextual* as a kind of dynamic that operated beneath the surface of classroom life but had great influence on children's work in school. It is hoped these ideas will enable the reader to see the children in this book and the dynamics of their social work without the encumbrances of social, psychological, and political labels. And perhaps they will provide frameworks for the reader to look again with new eyes at his or her own classroom or social community.

The reader should also know that because I customarily teach children for two continuous years, my thinking reflects an extended period of observation and reflection both as a teacher and as a teacher researcher; that the classroom I describe places a heavy value on the importance of uncovering children's thinking and their understanding of the world; that that classroom is not a place where children sit in rows and speak only when questioned, but is a moving, changing entity; and that I view the process of teaching and learning as an endeavor that teacher and child *mutually* negotiate.

As a result I see and hear things that are not available to researchers who collect data in other people's classrooms on designated days and for limited periods of time. The children and I are together for 180 days a year, seven hours a day. As their teacher, what I see most often is children working hard to understand their world and act upon it as social beings. Certainly on the surface they appear to be engaged in subject matter and mastering academic skills, but the real work of the classroom is social and subtextual. Learning is important to them, but finding and maintaining a place in their social milieu, gaining the attention and respect of their friends, is much more important.

To bring that world to life, I present the voices and the actions of specific children using both my field notes, or written observations of actual classroom events, and the children's words from audiotapes and verbatim texts. Within my field notes, I also incorporate my immediate responses to their words and actions when I describe an incident. Those responses are deliberately self-conscious because of my understanding that I, too, am a player in their performances, bringing in my own gender persona, my own cultural encumbrances, and my own influence as a co-actor.

As a teacher researcher, when I begin to examine closely children's words and actions, they always take on an element of great drama. I find my students' play, conversations, and interactions tremendously compelling, and after watching children for several years I believe it is important to uncover classroom dynamics that usually remain obscure in most studies of teaching and learning. For example, I have seen the effects of physical beauty on a child's behavior, have noted how some children play with the idea of being the other sex, and have tracked the alliances of silent girls. At all points, though, I want to make it clear that each of the children presented here is physically and emotionally healthy, and they are all genuinely trying to figure out what is a very complicated scenario, as am I. It is outside my scope to project why they do what they do or to draw hypothetical profiles of their home lives to account for the dilemmas they create. As a student of children's meanings, I find it more profitable to reflect upon the dynamics of the moment, because that is where understandings and misunderstandings are *mutually* negotiated, and that is where I, like the children, have agency, effect, and responsibility.

When children assume personae, their behavior is socially motivated. They make choices and orchestrate outcomes that do not necessarily reflect deep personal convictions. Rather, they are experimenting in the laboratory of the classroom, and the outcomes of their experiments give them data that they also reflect upon and use to determine the kinds of choices they want to make in the future. These children provide us with a mirror within which to contemplate both how they approach and negotiate the murky world of social relations, and how we, as adults, are approaching it. It is sometimes a disturbing reflection for us to consider, but it is always a provocative one.

CHAPTER 1

Teacher Research:
Texts and Subtexts

To teach as an art would require us to study the tranferences we bring to the world we know, to build our pedagogics not only around our feeling for what we know but also around our knowledge of why and how we have come to feel the way we do about what we teach. Then, perhaps, teaching the text may lead us to devise new forms for knowing that will not compel our students to recite the history and future of our desire.

—Grumet (1988)

What the ethnographer is in fact faced with . . . is a multiplicity of complex conceptual structures, many of them superimposed or knotted into one another, which are at once strange, irregular, and inexplicit, and which he must contrive somehow first to grasp and then to render. . . . Doing ethnography is like trying to read . . . a manuscript—foreign, faded, full of ellipses, incoherencies, suspicious emendations, and tendentious commentaries, but written not in conventionalized graphs of sound but in transient examples of shaped behavior.

—Geertz (1973)

Teaching is fundamentally a political activity in which every teacher plays a part by design or by default.

—Cochran-Smith (1991)

For some time now, I have been puzzled as to why I began tracking the manifestations of gender in my classroom. That sleuthing seemed to emerge as a preoccupation in 1990, when I began to think about how to manage bad boys. Then, the following year, I encountered Rachel, the most silent child I had ever met, and she presented me with management problems that rivaled those of the bad boys. I focused on her silence in order to work with her. That study turned into two years of thinking about girls and silence.

At the same time I found myself writing down everything that seemed to fit under the gender category. By 1992, well after my first writing on the topic, I was full tilt into watching every aspect of gender that made itself visible to me during the school day. Then, the next thing I knew, notations about race and class were going in my gender book, and by that time the whole process was very murky because by adding in new categories I was violating what had seemed to be a clear study of gender. Then I realized that when I was watching and taking field notes on sharing time, I was seeing instances of how gender or a child's home culture shaped that time; and finally every category of observation—and they were quite numerous—began to more closely resemble the mixed-up gender entries. I was immersed in a study, but I couldn't say exactly why or what meaning it had; the links and ties to curriculum and the craft of teaching were elusive, although I had always had the conviction that they were there. But what I was witnessing was so clearly social work; the forging of alliances and relationships; experimentations with power, attraction, and avoidance. It operated both inside and outside the boundaries of official classroom business, dynamically weaving a path throughout every aspect of our day. I knew this from the beginning as I traced the ways in which bad boys and silent girls impeded my teaching, but as the boundaries of what I was following became messy and blurred at the edges, I lost my own ability to see where I was going. I perceived that I was clearly working on a question, but what question was it?

TEACHERS' QUESTIONS

I believe it is a characteristic of teachers' questions that they often take the form of an observation that is steeped in the prosaics, the dailiness, of classroom life. The observation will be completely contextual and will be presented as an anecdote. For example, consider the following observation from my field notes:

> Denzel and I have a problem: he won't listen to story. Won't look at the pictures, either. This just makes me crazy. He's a good little kid and I can't for the life of me engage him in storytime, no matter what book we use or what devices I muster.

To an outsider, such an entry might seem to reflect either something wrong with the child or something wrong with my teaching. My anecdote clearly isn't complete enough. But the observation and the fact that I noticed it embody a question.

Teachers' questions are obscured by their contextuality, by being immersed in a particular "moment" of classroom or school time. They can seem trivial or unformed and usually are interpreted by others as a call for help, or something to be fixed. Both teachers and outsiders respond with explanations of the phenomenon, and solutions. "Well," they say, "why don't you try this?" or, "Have you read that?" or, "That's happened to me, and here's what I did." Observations that place problems of teaching and learning in the foreground seem to beg for a solution, but the solutions of others, however well intentioned, are rarely effective. They embody the widely held opinion that if teachers only knew enough about their craft, they wouldn't have messy questions that clearly represented a problem with a teacher's methodology or a child's deficits. The solutions also represent an approach to teaching that portrays classroom problems and teachers' questions as entities that can be remedied by tapping a general, all-purpose store of knowledge about teaching and learning, regardless of the unique nature of that classroom's students, physical space, materials, and teacher.

THE PROSAIC CLASSROOM

The origin of observations that embody questions is important to examine. As Bakhtin pointed out, the unfolding of the ordinary events of daily life, *of prosaics*, have much to offer us by way of understanding a language, a culture, a social milieu (Morson & Emerson, 1990). Observations that describe points of rupture in the life of the classroom, points of confusion, missteps, and even chaos give us access to the points when teacher intention as it is embodied in a method encounters the prosaic world of children and daily life. What Bakhtin called the "unfinalizability" of human discourse (see Morson & Emerson, 1990) is captured in such moments: the understanding that each new human encounter cannot rely on past scripts but rather must be freshly, and mutually, constructed in the moment. When we begin to expect teaching and learning moments to reproduce themselves as they are described in a book or recalled from prior successes, we are simplifying the process of human communication, making it static and dead, and pretending that it occurs without reference to each individual's past, present, and perceived future.

An emphasis on prosaics—on the dailiness, the mundane, the rupture—elevates considerations of language and culture to a role of dominance. It forces teachers to become researchers of children's meanings and views those meanings as being constructed within the unique point in history in which a class of children congregates with a particular teacher. Methodology is not discarded, but it is never viewed as the key or the sure path to a cohesive, smoothly operating classroom. The prosaic classroom is constantly shifting, and the teacher within it sees those shifts and brings to awareness her observations of that movement. Thus the problematic moment, as embodied in my earlier description of Denzel and storybooks, signals that an assumption or a method must be called into question as a point of common knowledge and investigated to uncover the layers of meanings it represents.

The Value of Confusion

> *At the center of fieldwork one confronts silence—a silence beyond language.*
> *—Becker (1992, p. 116)*

As I've tried to figure out why I pursued the tracks of gender, it seemed important to trace my interest back as far as I could remember. My first notes on what appeared to be a gender-related behavior in the classroom came when I was focusing on the development of sharing time in a class of children, one year before I met the children in this book. As I wrote at the time,

> After a while . . . I noticed the reactions of some of my Caucasian boys to Jiana's narratives . . . one day as I was observing their reactions very closely, I noticed their discomfort as she began. They looked at one another, began private conversations, and two in the front row turned their bodies away from her as she spoke. Joel said to the children around him, who were laughing at the narrative, "This isn't funny," and he lay down on the floor (Gallas, 1994, pp. 27–28).

The following year I began to think about bad boys, but it is clear that this earlier observation of Caucasian boys and an African American girl, an event that lasted no more than 30 seconds, embodied the question that I have pursued ever since, one that I can articulate only by asking all the questions that surround it: What did that behavior mean? What were those boys thinking? Why were they so blatantly disrespectful of Jiana when they were always respectfully treated by the other children in the class? What did the other children think? Was Jiana intimidated? Should I have chastised them? How could I have persuaded them to be respectful, to let themselves listen to her stories? What were their stories like? What did that behavior mean?

These questions circled around the anecdote, trying to find a way into the meaning of it. But it was the impression, the flavor, the intuition of the observation that remained immediate for me yet made my question difficult to home in on. And later, when I began watching, I saw that event repeated in different forms and contexts by different children in different years over and over again, always with the same charged impression. But still, what did it mean? What was the point of watching for it? What did it have to do with the process of teaching and learning?

Since 1988 I have been a member of the Brookline Teacher Research Seminar, a group that meets weekly to present and discuss data from our classrooms. It is a characteristic of our work that we don't always know what's going on. That seems, of course, like a terrible thing for teachers to admit, but it really is one of the underpinnings of the group's process and is certainly an admission predated by teacher writers in earlier decades, most especially in the work of Ashton-Warner (1963). As teacher researchers, we know what we use as our data: talk, field notes, classroom artifacts, personal journals. We know why we do that, and we know how to go about it, but we don't necessarily know in the beginning (and in my case, even for several years, as is now becoming plain) why we choose particular segments of talk, anecdote, drawing, or writing as data to bring to the group, or what our questions about them are. Often we just come with the explanation that "something is going on and I don't really know what it is, but here's something really interesting that I saw yesterday at recess."

We might characterize this experience of a puzzling event as a point of apprehension accompanied by a humbling declaration: standing in the middle of a situation that is clearly out of control, I say to no one in particular, "You guys, what the heck is going on here?" There is a deep silence within the cacophony that surrounds me. No one answers. This declaration is a response to confusion that I've spoken about before (Gallas, 1994), and it embodies a research position and a desire to understand, rather than a search for solutions. In other words, if we don't immediately know what's going on, then the problem is certainly worth investigating.

BUILDING DIALOGIC COMMUNITIES

An approach to teaching, learning, and research that values uncertainty and unfinalizability often results in a classroom milieu in which children have opportunities to build dialogic communities (Bakhtin, 1981, 1984), or classroom neighborhoods (Dyson, 1993). These communities represent a melding of many cultural viewpoints and are collectively constructed in the classroom, incorporating the "unofficial worlds" of children's lives into the flow of the "official world" of school (Dyson, 1993, p. 66). They are changeable and malleable communities whose concerns are often played out sociodramatically in response to the social and personal agendas of children. They are never duplicated as social microcosms, and their histories can never be predicted. And they are also potentially a modern day Pandora's box.

As a teacher researcher who made a place for unofficial worlds to enter the classroom, I have been able to view children's social discourse as a living, growing, and often uncensored body of action. My focus as a teacher researcher opened up the box, as it were, both unleashing something I could not always control, but also bringing the powerful (and ever present) dynamics of gender and race directly into the center of classroom life. Those dynamics and my participation in them changed children and the ways they viewed themselves and their classroom, changed our curricular agendas, and changed me. I began to see the "transference" Madeleine Grumet speaks about, understanding that children are not reconstructing my knowledge of the world and my "desire," but are rather attempting to "devise new forms for knowing" that were not available to me as a child (1988, p. 128).

From the vantage point of my classroom practices, I found my original investigations into classroom language prompted me to create distinct times in the day and week when children, not teachers, would orchestrate both formal and informal occasions to talk together. Those times took the form of sharing time, science talks, and morning art journals, and the children knew I would rarely appropriate those times for my own purposes. However, with that knowledge came risks, and perhaps even perils. I began to witness interactions and conversations that I didn't like, either for their intent or their content. I struggled to define how I should participate in those times and finally I decided that I should just participate as a member of the community. As I did so, I realized that my role was not to change what the children were doing and violate the space I had given them, but rather to try and make sense of what was happening within those child-orchestrated times, whether I liked what was happening or not. As a member of the Brookline Seminar, I found my reaction was not "I hate this behavior that I've unloosed, so now how do I change it?" but rather "What is going on here?" That still didn't lead me to the question I was investigating, but it allowed me to wait until my lack of understanding began to resolve itself—not in answers, but in an ability to see the children's patterns over time.

SEARCHING FOR PATTERNS

The ethnographer 'inscribes' social discourse, he writes it down. In so doing he turns it from a passing event, which exists only in its moment of occurrence, into an account which exists in its inscriptions and can be reconsulted.
—*Geertz (1973, p. 19)*

The patterns emerged in the process of collecting data and reflecting on it through writing. Data collection spanned five years and incorporated material from the classroom and playground, including observations, audiotapes, and field notes of children during formal and informal classroom events, interviews with children, samples of their writing and artwork, their performances and narratives. However, even after I had finished collecting data, I was not sure what I was seeing. The patterns I now see emerged only after a full year of writing and thinking, during which time I read, reviewed, and reconsidered my data. This was a year in which I did not teach and so had an unusual amount of time to do this work. What I learned during that year also proceeded in stages, each of which helped me to come to see the patterns in the children's social work, and to see also the patterns of my own social legacy.

Interpretation Versus Description

In the first stage, I naively began working with the data and writing about it as I often had for past projects. However, after three months, I was noticeably disoriented and disturbed by what I was writing and had actually made very little progress in figuring out what was going on. At the point in late December when I got locked out of my house not once, but twice in the same day, my husband very perceptively ordered me to stop writing and try to get a grip on what was happening. It is a tribute to his understanding of me and the work I had been doing that when he did so, I meekly (and uncharacteristically) did exactly as he told me and did not attempt to work on the data again until February. By then I felt I had stepped back a bit, and I began to see that what was disturbing me was not what I had observed in the classroom for four years, but rather, *my interpretation* of those observations. I was ascribing to the children motives that were distinctly those of adults; they were my motives, reflecting my understanding of the world. In other words, I wasn't making *their* sense, I was making my own sense, based on how I perceived interactions around race and gender usually proceeded in society at large.

I went back to work on the writing for a brief period but was still troubled as to how to present the descriptions of what I had seen without placing a negative interpretation on them. It seemed to me that I was still unable to see the children clearly. Fortunately, before I began to lock myself out of the house again, I stopped writing while I did some traveling. In April, I returned once again to the work. By this time, I had somehow come to a new level of understanding that occurred outside the writing process. (I think it is important to point out here that my account of this first stage of writing highlights problems inherent in the process of teacher research.

Teacher researchers have very little time for extended reflection and writing, if they are classroom teachers. The understandings that I came to in relation to this project occurred over a twelve-month period *in which I did not teach*.)

Reading Classroom Topography

What I had previously seen as sad and disturbing stories of children's mistreatment of each other I was now able to see as children trying to figure out the uncharted social terrain that I had so graciously turned over to them. Each player in the daily drama, including me, now became a performer who was trying to figure things out based on his or her knowledge of that classroom terrain, and my purpose was to describe their performances. That metaphor, of children finding their way, enabled me to begin to follow their trails through that terrain—to create a map of how social relations unfold when the topography is not laid out and controlled by a well-meaning adult.

And what did I see? I saw children, each with a unique perspective from which they made forays into the social life of the classroom. I also saw that that perspective was a dynamic one that developed in direct response to the reactions of their classmates and me. Sometimes that perspective and their performance of it would change from week to week; at other times it would remain static and they would be stuck in a role. However, the children were always (as I was) trying to make sense of the classroom culture, to see patterns, to find their way and define who they were or wanted to be, to penetrate ways of being that were not always familiar to them but that they desired to understand. I began to see their efforts as forming a body of energy that ran beneath the more visible events that structured their day. The daily instructional routines of language arts, reading, science, math, gym, music, art, and lunch went on like a preordained ritual that seemed to shape what our lives in school meant. But beneath that comfortable structure was the *real* life of the classroom. It was submerged but powerful, and in different ways it permeated all our work with more formal classroom texts: with my efforts to help children reach for and appropriate those texts, and with the children's motivation and efforts to do so.

TEXTS AND SUBTEXTS

Beneath the surface of classroom life are what I now call the *subtextual dynamics of classroom life*. These dynamics represent the impression and the flavor that I spoke of earlier; they represent the vital undercurrents in the classroom, those conditions that are not given a priori when children and teachers gather to learn. And they often cannot be simply and neatly portrayed. They are in direct contrast to the "texts" that embody the goals of schooling, even as they interact with those texts. Here "text" is interpreted broadly as "any coherent complex of signs" (Bakhtin, 1986, p. 103), a definition that shaped my earlier work on narrative, or story (Gallas, 1994).

For teachers and children, a text to be considered in the classroom can be a book, a child's story, a painting, a song, a poem, a dance, a slide under a microscope, a mathematical formula, an experiment. The subtextual, however, defies reification as a text because it is about the vitality of daily life among children. It reflects what Edith Cobb (1994) identified as "worldmaking," the points at which the child attempts to reconcile the outer (textual) worlds of his or her reality with inner worlds of reflection and imagination. At the same time the subtextual continuously comes in contact with the texts of the classroom, or the curriculum, and society at large, and deeply influences how (or even whether) a child approaches those texts. The sense that children make of classroom texts, their interpretation of them, their behavior at points of contact, then, are the embodiment of the subtextual. This sense is made visible in their talk, stories, and gestures, and even in their silences.

Reifying the Subtextual

As a teacher researcher, when I audiotape, transcribe, and take field notes in the classroom, I am essentially reifying the subtextual work of the children, bringing what is veiled into my line of vision. At that point, the children's social work, their efforts to bring their lives into contact with the curricula I present, become texts that I can make contact with, can "reconsult." Yet as a teacher whose process of worldmaking is bound by my own life experiences, my experience of the children's texts and the ways I anticipate they will be received and interpreted by their peers are limited. I cannot anticipate the vagaries of children's responses to what might seem to be a straightforward teaching or learning event. Not every child is like me, nor are they like my experience of my own children. Those who are like me are more easily figured out; I can predict their reactions, and I often naively suppose that every other child will react similarly. But then the rupture occurs: my expectation that what has been successful in the past will be so in the future is overturned. Thus my bewilderment over Denzel's resistance to storybooks, my uneasiness with the boys' refusal to listen to Jiana.

The construct of the subtextual enables me to see the dynamic life beneath the texts that anchor my curricula, to perceive their permeability and that their value and meanings are completely subjective for each member of the classroom. But it is only through the action of classroom research that I can give shape and form to the children's subtextual work, that I can begin to map the terrain they are trying to negotiate and see the topography of our classroom culture. As Grumet points out,

> curriculum, like language, is a moving form; conceived as an aspiration, the object and hope of our intentionality, it comes to form and slips, at the moment of its actualization, into the ground of our action. It becomes part of our situation (1988, p. 131)

Like language, curriculum is negotiated in contact with the intentions of others, but teachers do not always see how their work in teaching texts comes in contact with those intentions. It is only in the identification of ruptures, of confusion, and of puzzling behaviors, and in the dogged pursuit of the subtexts which surround those, that our teaching moves from reproduction into art.

Collecting the Subtexts

This work did not start out with any notion of classroom topography or the subtextual. It began with what appeared to be many discreet observations on my part, and an approach one might describe as alternately befuddled, amused, and outraged. I was a collector and a reactor: I collected indiscriminately and reacted quite personally to what I gathered. It was very much like an aesthetic exercise: some things pleased me, some repelled; all fascinated.

The next chapter will present some of the kinds of things I collected in the process of giving form to the subtextual. It will ease the reader into a consideration of how children "do" gender and other social work, beginning with a description of what I call the "gender circus." It is what I saw when I first began to look, and it represents what a visitor to my classroom might see on any given day, a slice of "prosaics," as it were. Later chapters will add on to this first general look by focusing on different players in the classroom as they diversify their roles and bring their lives to bear on the development of their classroom community. As we move more deeply into those descriptions, the points of contact between what we call "school" and children's desires to map their social terrain will become more visible and more complex.

CHAPTER 2

The Gender Circus

In ordinary experience we're all in the position of a dog in a library, surrounded by a world of meaning in plain sight that we don't even know is there.
—*Frye (1964, p. 79)*

One spring morning a few years ago, I asked myself a question that, oddly, after more than 20 years of teaching, had just occurred to me: Why had I chosen to spend so many years of my life in a classroom sequestered for most of the day with young children, half of whom often seemed like aliens? The aliens I speak of were the little boys in my class of first and second graders, and what had suddenly become clear was my realization that the very essence of their beings was a mystery to me. At that particular moment in school time my little boys had temporarily taken over the classroom, staging a sort of minor coup. This was a routine event that usually happened several times each day and was always accompanied by noise (something I really hate), milling around, flailing of arms, and other forms of anarchy.

I realized, in that brief moment of clarity, that what had once seemed routine and mundane was, in fact, peculiar. It was peculiar that, for the purposes of education, twenty or more children, all of the same age, would be confined for several hours a day in a room with a woman as their sole caretaker. Then, to streamline the process, several of those rooms were grouped together in one building with (usually) a man as the leader, and this unnatural arrangement of people and rooms was called A SCHOOL.

Now, I would not want anyone to think this was the first time that the oddity of "school" had presented itself to me. But what flashed before me at this point in my history as a teacher was the peculiarity of *my* position in the classroom. I saw that my gender put me in a strange place. There I was, sitting in a classroom surrounded by behaviors that I considered to be bizarre, but they were bizarre only because I was female. Further, I returned happily to this circus day after day, with true curiosity about the shenanigans I might yet see. Essentially, because of the peculiar environment of the school, I found myself in the middle of a virtual laboratory of gender. There, at any time of the day, I could see, hear, and document instances of children trying on different roles, events that took place with intensity and regularity precisely because we were all confined in that room together.

I began to reflect on what made that particular moment so odd. I was sitting in a small chair meant for 6- or 7-year-olds, surrounded by a few standing children who were waiting for me to look at their journals. As I read each journal and spoke to each child, I could see that there were pieces of paper flying from one part of the room to the other. A little boy's head popped up quickly to assess the accuracy of the shot, then popped back down when he saw me watching him. To my left, I noticed a table of boys beginning to make snorting pig noises as they wrote, each boy's effort raising the level of volume as well as the calling up of more phlegm. I returned to my discussion with the students around me and realized that they were all little girls. They stood patiently, watching me watch the class, waiting serenely until I returned to their journals. I sighed—a deep, resigned, and wistful sigh. The little girls looked sympathetic, and for a moment I wondered what it would be like to teach in a classroom where every child was like these peaceful, studious girls. It was only a fleeting thought, but the sigh told everything.

For me, the watchword in the classroom is "calm." I feel that everything is going well if students have an appearance of calm and purpose. That doesn't mean that there won't also be activity, movement, initiative, excitement, independence, and talk, but underneath it all will be calm, purpose, and order. (Notice how the adjectives begin to multiply.) Obviously, then, what I mind most as a teacher is the loss of calm—in other words, turmoil. Turmoil means pandemonium and confusion—and noise (different from talk), running (different from movement, at least in a classroom space), unfettered physicality (meaning wrestling, pushing, hitting, maybe even spitting), and random activity. These are all things young boys do well. I guess I had realized with a shock that deep in my heart, contrary to all my talk about androgyny and overcoming stereotypes, I was still corralled by my gender; many of my preferences for the way my students *ought* to be were female preferences, but half of my students were male.

Well, I can't help it, it's just the way I am. But to be truthful, although I can easily forgive my pervasive female nature because I spend so much time trying to moderate it in my teaching, I still feel bad for the boys who walk into my classroom as first graders. I know that their lives, as they have known them, are about to end. Inside the school and within a classroom, these poor, once carefree children have to be "civilized." They can't run, wrestle, roll, push, spit, hit, or produce bloodcurdling screams.

As their teacher, I have to help them begin to contain themselves. It is a sad sight to see when they realize what's happening. Some of them immediately rebel, and in fact, as this book will show, continue to rebel at every possible opportunity. Others are able to accept my authority and the reasons I give them to justify their containment, but it hurts them. In fact, they sometimes seem as if they are in physical pain from being denied the ability to move constantly. A few gym periods a week don't help, and even 30 minutes a day of running at recess provides only temporary relief. No matter that they can have some freedom of movement within the classroom; sitting long enough to hear a story can be a form of torture.

But the girls, if they suffer from their introduction to school, don't show it. Sitting and listening for long periods of time is not hard for most of them. Working quietly on a project actually satisfies them. Taking turns talking suits their way of communicating. They are appalled at their male classmates, who shout out, push, run, step on them, and regularly lose control. The sight of a six-year-old girl watching two 7-year-old boys wrestling in the middle of storytime is something to behold. She is aghast at the ridiculous spectacle and will tell the wrestlers so, but rather than intervening and joining the fracas, as her male counterparts inevitably do, she sits waiting, sighing heavily and shrugging her shoulders.

I feel pretty much the same. It saddens me to see little boys who are so often at the mercy of their nervous systems. They almost twitch with uncontrollable energy. On other days, however, I feel sad for my little girls. Most of them take the safe road. They quietly watch, listen, and study every nuance of the classroom so that they won't make mistakes in public. They are very proud and would rather remain silent than lose face by offering a new idea. Some, paralyzed by fear of failure, become passive and risk nothing. At those times I long to extract a bit of bravado from the boys, most of whom have not even conceived that risk taking is dangerous, and mix it with the girls' passive wistfulness. Then I look around me at the erupting chaos, and I want to take the girls' composure and neural integration and inject it into my hurtling boys.

Most of the time, though, it's all a muddle. Boys and girls each need some of what the others have, but unfortunately, the traits boys and girls bring into school are not of the mix-and-match variety. You take what they bring and begin to work with it, hoping in the process to offer them opportunities to try on different ways of being in the world. What they bring, however, is very distinctive. For example, consider the following observations that were taken from my journals over a 2-year period.

SNAPSHOTS FROM THE CIRCUS

November 24: 8:00 A.M.

Rachel comes to class wearing a beautiful rose-covered dress. Her long black hair is loose to her waist, and she's carrying a blue beret with a rose on the front. Her mother whispers to me that Rachel, who usually wears pants or jeans, wanted to wear the dress but is very self-conscious. I see that she is self-conscious but also very aware of the beauty of the dress. Mia arrives and walks toward the group of girls who are admiring Rachel's dress. She is wearing a horizontally striped black and white skirt over a thick purple sweatshirt. She goes directly over to Rachel and comments on how beautiful the dress is, then says how her sister wore her (Mia's) dress to daycare because she was wearing her sister's skirt to school. They had made a trade for the day.

Then Mia launches into a description of her own dress, mentioning the sleeves (lace), and that it had "stripes and roses all around, and up and down," and as she says this, she twirls around twice, pointing to show where the roses are, "and," she says of her sister, "she wore lipstick, too." The girls (and, I have to confess, my intern and I) are all delighted with her story. We can picture Mia's sister, dressed and lipsticked, and when Mia is told by one of the other girls that Rachel is shy about her dress, she says with great surprise, "Why? You look so beautiful!"

Ten minutes later we have gathered for sharing time, and Michael takes his turn. He pulls four comic books out of a bag: *Conan the Barbarian*; *Jimm, Son of Saturn*; *Spider Man Unlimited, Maximum Carnage*; and *Battle Tide II, Death's Head and Kill Power*. He shows the comic books and takes questions and comments, and only the boys participate. Then he says, "I have a question for you. What does 'carnage' mean?" Three boys say they know, but no one in class, including those boys, will volunteer an answer.

Michael asks, "Do you want a hint?"

The children nod. He continues, "It's sort of, in a way, has to do with cutting."

Two boys make fruitless guesses, and Michael adds, "It's sort of cutting, like cutting things, shooting out and cutting things."

Immediately, two boys begin to tussle and make shooting noises. I ask them to calm down, but they continue to roll and wrestle and shoot. For the next five minutes, as we try to carry on, we hear pops and whooshes, kind of like little firecrackers going off in the background. Alexis gets in the chair to take her turn sharing and shows a book, *The Story of the First Thanksgiving*. The boys settle down and refocus, and gradually the popping sounds fade away.

January 5: 12:30 P.M.

We are working on a social studies lesson, and Rachel looks up as I walk by, smiles dreamily to herself, and says, "I can't wait until we make our Valentine's boxes." She smiles again and goes back to work. I continue to stare at her and wonder where that came from. Valentine's Day is over a month away.

Thirty minutes later, as I move around the room assisting children with their math work, Michael looks up at me, smiling that same dreamy smile, and says, "Karen, will we swim again this year?" (referring to a swimming trip that we take in June!). I answer in the affirmative and wonder again about the sources of these children's musings. Both are ostensibly working on assigned projects; each is reminiscing about an activity from the year before and daydreaming about its reoccurrence this year. What doesn't surprise me is the difference in their choices of a treasured memory.

Sharing Time: January 25

Dierdre brings a rubberband ball in for sharing. She explains how she and her father made the ball and tells the class how they have been collecting rubberbands for a long time. We can see that: The ball is bigger than a softball. She asks for questions and comments, but only the boys and Josie (the tom boy) respond, and they do so with great admiration and enthusiasm for about five minutes. None of the girls but Josie has anything to ask or say.

Mia takes her turn to share and pulls out some photographs of her family. The girls all sit up and look lively. Rachel gets up from the back row and moves to a space directly in front of Mia's knees. She looks up at Mia with a bright, unwavering smile on her face. The girls ask many questions and make Mia show certain pictures again. The boys also participate and point out their favorites.

Finally, John takes his turn and announces he will share a mystery. This is a genre that the boys in the class invented last year. They provide a crime or an event and ask a question, for example, "Sophie and John are found dead in their room. There is broken glass and water all over the floor. How did they die?" Then the children in the audience have 15 chances to guess the answer. They can either ask yes-or-no questions or make guesses. (The correct answer for this mystery: Sophie and John were goldfish, and the cat knocked over the bowl.) John describes the mystery for today and asks for questions and guesses. None of the girls but Josie asks questions or participates in guessing; *all* the boys do. By this time I am very irked. Anytime risks or critical thinking are involved, these little girls are absolutely passive. I wonder if we need single-sex schools.

The First Day of Spring: March 22

My class is out of control. Actually, the boys are out of control: they are milling around, pinching bottoms (their own and the girls'), chasing, running, and generally losing both physical and mental control all day. The girls, however, are fine: calm, and very focused on their work. After asking the boys what is going on and receiving dazed stares in reply, I huddle with the girls, figuring maybe they know what's going on. They report to a person that the boys are "girl crazy":

DIERDRE: It's like they can't leave us alone. They chase and pinch and tease.
JOSIE: And they can't even play right anymore. They just tease instead of playing. Like when we play birds and raptors, only Andy can play. The rest are too silly.

Morning Meeting: May 18

Eli and Germaine, two of the littlest and youngest boys in the class, have brought handkerchiefs to school, and Eli has tied his red one around his head like a "skater." Germaine keeps trying to do the same during sharing time, but his handkerchief is smaller and keeps falling off. Germaine scrutinizes the back of Eli's head, trying to figure out, I think, how to get his to stay on.

Since the beginning of the year I have outlawed the wearing of hats of any kind in the classroom, both baseball and otherwise, based on my understanding of how hats are used by bad boys to create certain effects in their interactions with teachers. (That is insider information I got from my son when he was still in high school and had developed a sophisticated practical understanding of such things. Bad boys learn quite early that simply by changing the angle and tilt of their hat they can alter the dynamics of a conversation with a teacher. For example, if a boy is being defiant or evasive, he'll very deftly tap the top of his brim and lower it so that the teacher can't see his eyes. At the same time, he'll slouch further down in his chair, lean back, and tilt his head to the side. Essentially, he takes control of the eye contact. There are other variations on this theme.)

These little boys, however, have found a way to get around my no-hat rule: A scarf is not a hat, just as a headband is not a hat. All through the meeting Germaine is unable to do anything but try and tie the handkerchief. Finally I tie it for him. I have to admit that he and Eli do look very cool. As I casually glance around the class, I note that none of the girls are wearing anything that strictly defines them as girls. In fact, the only identifying characteristic is the length of the children's hair. For the most part, all the children wear the same sort of clothing: pants, t-shirts, and sneakers. The colors of the clothing do have some variation in that girls tend to wear more shades of pink and purple, but the design of the clothing of all the children is for comfort. Only on special, dressy occasions such as school picture day or a performance will the girls wear dresses or skirts. At those times, some boys will also add a tie and jacket.

Each of these excerpts represents no more than one 30-minute period in a school day, and in some cases, less than a five-minute period of observation. All throughout each day, day by day, week by week, month by month, these young children show me very contrasting ways of being in the world. I have learned that what they bring to school, the things that give them pleasure, their interests and passions, are often strongly differentiated according to gender. After many years I realized that in order to teach them better, I needed to know more about those differences and the points at which they either furthered or hindered their growth as learners.

As I watched, I also began to see the points at which my category of gender blurred and moved into other social domains, and interactions where some children crossed over the boundaries of gender and met on common ground. The following chapters will expand the first impressions that these snapshots provide, introducing children and the performances they engaged in on a daily basis, and deliberately adding more layers and more complexity to our picture of how boys and girls relate to the world. The snapshots, however, are where this process of trying to understand children's social work began. They were, from my point of view as a teacher researcher, how my process of data collection began. As the reader will see, however, these first impressions become much more complicated as my ability to focus in develops, and as the children's efforts to make themselves visible to others become more public. In many ways, the fact that I am watching and what I am able to see grow in direct proportion to the children's realization that I *am* watching and listening and desiring to know how they understand their world.

CHAPTER 3

Bad Boys and Their Stories

Born "rebels" who defy authority are not oblivious to it but oversensitive to it. Defying authority is a way of asserting themselves and refusing to accept the subordinate position.

—Tannen (1990, p. 291)

This chapter enables the reader to consider with me how power is defined in the classroom. It describes the natural authority some children brought to my classroom, and how that authority set a climate for much of what happened throughout the days, months, and years we were together. It will begin to illustrate that the "power assymetry" described by Edwards and Mercer (1987) is only partially in the hands of the teacher, and in many ways is more clearly within the control of small numbers of influential children. In my classroom, those children were male, Caucasian, and privileged. The story of my journey deeper into the territory of the gender circus begins with bad boys, a small but influential group that first captured my attention as they boldly and effectively sought to control the social and instructional climate of the classroom.

Sharing Time: November 3

MICHAEL: Then Hades came along with Zeus. Then Charles came along as one of the nine muses. They're all girls.
CHARLES: I'd rather be a midget than that.
MICHAEL: Then you're not going to come in my story for a long time. You'll be a Minotaur.
CHARLES: A midget.
MICHAEL: A midgetor, half bull, half lady. So me and Zeus, the Hydra, and Hades, all went to Crete. And that's where we all got taken to prison. But Zeus broke us out, and we all went inside the Minotaur's, excuse me, the Midgetor's maze.

Once again Michael began his Wednesday morning with an amazing story in which only a few children in the class, most of them boys, could participate. Michael's friends, Charles, Andrew, and Daniel, had been avidly reading books on Greek mythology and regularly regaled each other with retellings of the stories. This time, however, with the whole class as the audience, Michael improvised on one of their favorites, using Charles as his foil, which absolutely delighted his friends. The other children, however, did not get the jokes and wordplay, but Michael, who only made eye contact with his three friends, didn't seem to care. That sharing chair was his, at least for a while, and he could use it to display his extensive mastery of language and to make it clear which children in the class were his friends. Michael was extremely articulate, providing continuous examples of how one creates social hierarchies using only words.

Michael was, from the time he entered first grade, a bad, sometimes very bad, little boy. He had had that reputation coming in from kindergarten and lost no time as a six-year-old living up to his reputation. (My first year with Michael is chronicled in more detail in my first book: Gallas, 1994, pp. 61–64. There is also a portrait of Charles in first grade: pp. 64–67.) In his first year with me, Michael, along with Charles and Andrew, joined two other notorious second grade-bad boys, Tony and Tom, and immediately became their disciple. Although Michael, Charles, and Andrew brought in a sturdy repertoire of bad boy behaviors, their apprenticeship with Tony and Tom rounded out their skills.

BAD BOYS AS A CARICATURE

"Bad boys" is a term I first developed to describe particular boys and the effect they had on the classroom. I use it as a caricature for how these boys view themselves and are viewed both by other children and by their teachers. In using the term my intention is to highlight their behavior while also underscoring the complexity of their motives. Bad boys are "bad" in the sense of the street lingo that they so admire and try to use: they are bad, meaning they push the boundaries of all behavioral norms, and they are also bad, meaning attractive, risky, desirable, cool. The construction of their personae, however, is a performance that conceals many layers of social awareness, creative activity, and ambivalence toward powerful others (usually, but not always, women).

In my experience, "bad" boys are usually Caucasian, from middle- or upper-middle-class homes, and highly articulate. In a class of twenty-four children, perhaps only one or two boys might fall into this category. Beginning as early as the kindergarten year, though, in spite of their small representation in a class, they can be extremely disruptive. Their main strategy for disruption revolves around a surprisingly sophisticated understanding and manipulation of language to control social interactions. They begin school using language to disrupt class discussion, playing on what a teacher or another child has said, using off-color references or sounds, crude gestures, or nonsense words. Their behavior is distracting and disrespectful of both teachers and other children in the class, and often offensive.

Usually these boys act as the critic of teachers, regardless of the subject, implying in their comments and nonverbal communication that the topics under study are boring and irrelevant to their lives. As Deborah Tannen points out, "the act of giving information by definition frames one in a position of higher status, while the act of listening frames one as lower. Children instinctively sense this, as do most men" (1990, p. 139). Bad boys, by having to listen to the teacher, feel the unequal status. They become well known throughout the school for their disruptive, pejorative behavior in every class (often including gym), and spend a great deal of time sitting outside the door of music, art, or gym classes or on the principal's bench. As they mature they become more sophisticated, learning that disruption and classroom control can be had with very few astutely placed words or even meaningless gestures whose tone to teachers and classmates is very obvious.

BAD BOYS AND POWER

In many ways these boys are the individuals in schools who, from an early stage, question the norms school represents. Their behavior, if it were only aimed at adults, might be seen as political, a rebellion over the status quo or a precocious questioning of the authority of schools. However, bad boys do not care about power only in relation to established authority figures like teachers or principals; they desire more of an encompassing social control, rather than political control. Thus children as well as adults can be the focus of their machinations; their goal in all things is to be superior to others, either by controlling the dynamics of interactions, or, if that isn't possible, by withholding their participation. Tannen points out that for men and boys, affiliation, friendship, and association often begin with aggressive behavior, while for girls it begins with association and support: "The point of affiliation (for boys) is power" (1990, p. 141). This dynamic exactly describes how bad boys begin their interactions in the classroom and why a class is so easily subdued and almost hypnotized by their behavior. Other boys see aggressive behavior, verbal or physical, as an overture to belonging. Girls see it as something to be amused by, not interfered with.

Privately, I know bad boys to be soft spoken, articulate, sensitive, and affectionate children. They often have creative talent and always enjoy a good, meaty discussion with an adult. Publicly, when they are being observed by their peers in the presence of an adult, they assume a critical, distant, somewhat superior air. When presented by teachers with what they consider to be repetitive and mundane work, they resist, regardless of the function of the exercise. In my experience they are most happy when studying "serious" subjects, or when working alone or with chosen friends on independent projects, especially art projects. At those times a bad boy's attention is diverted from his public self back into the private child.

Yet even if a teacher engages them intellectually or artistically, the social position these boys adopt is both a source of power and a trap. As Vivian Paley has observed, "The bad guy always promises more power—or more freedom—than the good guy" (1984, p. 23), and it is true that bad boys quickly become dominant in classrooms and are admired by less aggressive boys and popular girls. However, in the process of garnering this adulation, bad boys often cut themselves off from a deep engagement in learning and in their classroom community. The "bad boy" persona gives them prestige but isolates them from the community of the classroom. As they develop and refine their ability to use language to critique, judge, and embarrass, they also disrupt instruction, intimidate classmates, and force a code of detachment on themselves that denies their potential as learners and thinkers.

Sometimes bad boys are amusing and odd, especially if you're watching them surreptitiously, as I do. They are constantly looking for the edge in their relationships with others, figuring out how to gain the upper hand. When I watch them, I always wonder how they get to be the way they are. In a social encounter with other children they often expend a great deal of energy trying to get some small quotient of power and hold onto it. In many ways, as I've observed them, I can't help but see them as caricatures. It is as if I am watching a soap opera about powerful grown men portrayed in their most negative aspects, except that the performers are children. Where on earth did these young boys learn to act this way, and with such skill? Where did they learn to pontificate, interrupt, tease, and belittle without paying any (visible) social price? By first grade they are capable of complex and subtle social maneuvering, tampering with the edges of social acceptability while simultaneously making the rules for what is acceptable.

Repeatedly over the years, I have observed six-, seven-, and eight-year-old boys, who are very interested in power, figure out how to push the boundaries of public discourse so that they can always be at the top of the social hierarchy. Now, if you're just watching these guys and are outside their influence, as I sometimes am, you find their machinations both amazing and horrifying. They are amazing because of the level of Machiavellian intelligence they exhibit. They are horrifying both for that reason, and because of what they reveal about these children's understanding of modern society. At a very early age, these boys have an astonishing sense of how power is constructed to subdue and intimidate others, to control social dynamics, and to obtain special favors.

However, if you are a child who is the object of their machinations, of their rehearsal, as it were, for life, then you do not see them as odd or amusing; rather, they worry, threaten, intimidate, and yes, at times, silence you. In fact, when bad boys are practicing being bad and you are their idea of a good target, you're not really sure how you ought to react, so you just smile or keep quiet. Part of the reason for that is that no one around you seems to know what to do when these boys are doing their work. Regular, nice boys and girls, sometimes even your best friends, will go along with them, choosing to be quiet and watch rather than interfere and defend you. That's part of the bad boy's art: he makes you think that his attention, however threatening, might be a form of friendship or admiration.

Children, like most other people in this culture, are both fascinated by and afraid of bad boys. Bad boys fit into a special cultural niche, following in the footsteps of James Dean, Elvis Presley, Marlon Brando, and Mick Jagger. (All of us could add more names.) They are attractive and risky; speak softly, as if they are telling secrets; and say insinuating things to anyone they want while looking them straight in the eye. Sometimes they take your words and turn them around so you sound foolish. At other times they seem to like you, then use a few well-placed words to humiliate you.

In my experience these boys are experimenting with the character of the bad boy to see how it fits. They walk around in the character for a while and play with the kind of power it provides. But their experimentations do not necessarily mean that they are taking on a permanent bad boy persona. Many of them decide at some point that being a dominant boy in a room full of children and a school full of powerful adults is not as rewarding as they thought it would be; it requires a constant expenditure of energy to stay on top. For any number of reasons the role is not satisfying, and they move on to explore other ways of defining themselves. Other boys, however, find the social rewards too rich, the status too tempting, and the notoriety too stimulating to forgo.

BAD BOYS' STORIES

Bad boys usually use language to accomplish their goals, and often I could best see how they worked by observing them in sharing time. They preferred the genre of "fake stories" for their own storytelling and would often choose the public context of sharing to assert their social authority in the class. In many of the stories, their targets were the girls in the class, who were often collectively blown up or bombarded with objects, or were abandoned to an unknown fate on out-of-control airplanes. In contrast, if other boys or girls told stories that included many members of the class, generally the trouble in the story would be divided equally between boys and girls and would not be one of violence or humiliation.

I have witnessed stories told by bad boys in which every girl in the class, as well as rival boys, were physically punished in some way, and even I was occasionally beaten, maimed, or killed. Those kinds of stories, while couched in the "make-believe" mode, were threatening and disturbing to many children and to me. I had established a rule in sharing, after the bad boys repeatedly told violent stories, that people could not be killed or hurt in the stories. That rule had improved the tone of the stories, but the bad boys had found new ways to embellish their stories, so that the message of humiliation or threat was still intact but the words were not offensive. Although the effect was less aggressive, it still made certain children vulnerable, since very few children dare to object to their portrayal in a story. That kind of objection, and the attention it draws, might be more humiliating than the outcome of the story itself.

BAD BOYS AND OTHER CHILDREN'S STORIES

There was an unspoken rule among the children that you mustn't seem like you weren't glad to be in the stories told. That rule originally emerged, I think, to show solidarity with the storyteller. All the children knew that it was risky to sit up in the teacher's chair and tell a completely imaginary story. They all maintained the encouraging and supportive attitude of being glad when they were included in a new story, irrespective of the storyteller's skill. But of course, that rule didn't apply to the bad boys.

Sometimes, when another child started a story and was naming a cast of characters, the bad boys would say quite loudly that they didn't want to be in the story. Since so few children ever objected to being in a story, the bad boys' requests were usually honored. (In fact, I never observed *any* of the other children asking *not* to be included in a story.) Often, after they had stated their preference, the boys would very blatantly not listen to the story, talking among themselves or rolling on the floor. (The reader will recall my first glimpse of that behavior from Chapter 1.) Whose stories didn't they want to be in? In fact, that is a painful thing to relate, because their message was clear. The children they withheld consent from were outsiders—African-American children, Caucasian children who had low status in class but were trying to form alliances through their stories, children who were new English speakers, or children who threatened them: girls, like Dierdre or Mia, whom the bad boys had recently treated badly in their own stories, or other well-liked boys. Whose stories did they want to be in? That is a predictable answer: the stories of their close friends, stories that usually placed them as central and powerful characters who led others into trouble and mischief.

For example, Michael, as a first grader, would get in the chair week after week and tell stories that featured Tony, Tom, and Donald. If he and Charles were at odds, he would place Charles in a dangerous situation and annihilate him by the end of the story.

> Charles got to the top of a mountain, but fell off and was caught by Sarah (our cockatiel), who was also caught by an eagle, who was caught by a vulture, who took them to her nest, where Charles was almost eaten alive by the vulture and her babies. Charles landed in Crocodile Falls, where alligators swallowed him, and he burst into lots of little Charleses. Then Charles fell into the ocean, and everyone else—all the little Charleses—also fell in Crocodile Falls, but they had trouble getting out because they were all shrunk. The last we saw of Charles, he was floating in a coffin in the Pacific Ocean.

Charles, in second grade, had mastered the use of fake stories, and would tell stories that included only Michael, Andrew, and sometimes Daniel. When he told the stories, he made eye contact with those children as they smiled and laughed. One day in December I recorded the following in my field notes:

> Who is Charles talking to? He is looking directly at Andrew and no one else. Andrew is starting to chat back with suggestions and comments as Charles tells his story. Charles's eyes have not left Andrew's face. His gaze now moves to Michael as he begins to talk about him. Then, when he adds in Daniel, he looks at him as he talks. It's like the rest of us aren't here.

Finally, the class had a format for sharing time in which they could announce at the end of their story "To Be Continued." Usually, that signaled that they would continue telling the story the next week, and other children could also take up the story and add on to it, changing settings and adding characters. The bad boys, however, would begin a story that included only their friends, and then the next day one of those friends would take up the story and add on more, keeping only the same characters. Sometimes, if another child who was not in the story asked to continue their story, usually for the purpose of building an alliance with them, the boys would refuse.

There were other ploys to make plain their dominant place in the classroom. One day, for example, after Andrew performed a magic trick during sharing, Nathaniel raised his hand during the question-and-comment period. Andrew, however, would not acknowledge him. I prompted Andrew to call on everyone, and a bit later he pointed at Nathaniel and said, "I forget his name."

"No, you don't," I said with surprise.

"Oh, right, " responded Andrew, and he called Nathaniel by name.

Their stories were in direct contrast to the stories of the other children. For example, Ian, in introducing his story one day, began with this comment: "We're going on an Arctic trip. I'll try and mention everybody's name," and he proceeded to tell a story in which he did mention everyone, and put Daniel, then a new first grader, in a central role. Many children used their stories to build alliances rather than to separate themselves from others. Often, children who wanted to join a friendship group would tell a story about that group, putting the children in a central role and including themselves as a friend.

Maintaining Dominance

Not all the machinations of bad boys were so planned or so public as the stories told in sharing time. Sometimes the messages they delivered to other children were done covertly, or said under their breath. Being an eavesdropper of long standing, I developed a high-level ability to catch these mutterings and sometimes intervened. Often, however, my intervention meant nothing because I was not the object of the barb, and further, I couldn't see and hear every exchange. Such an incident occurred one morning before school started, as a few children sat in the meeting area, talking and waiting for everyone to arrive. Two girls were chatting casually about what they'd had for breakfast. I was standing in an adjacent area, looking through my notebooks. One girl said that she had eaten an English muffin. Germaine, an African American child who was sitting quietly by himself, turned to Andrew, who was sitting close by, and said, "What does an English muffin look like?" I glanced up, smiling. Germaine always maintained a serious interest in food.

Andrew looked directly at him without smiling and answered quietly, "Your ass."

Germaine did not visibly react and simply turned away, his curiosity effectively silenced. I was infuriated at the meanness of the remark and walked over to Andrew, knelt down beside him, and told him quietly what I thought of his answer. He looked down at his hands and his lips quivered. Then I asked him if he could give Germaine a real answer to his question. Andrew nodded and described in great detail what an English muffin was, and how it was different from a regular muffin. Germaine listened carefully and silently, then turned away.

But the deed was already done: Germaine had been humiliated. What was hurtful here was not so much what Andrew said as his intention. The tone of his response to Germaine wasn't the teasing or bantering tone he might have used with his friends; this was said with contempt and was intended to embarrass. There were no witnesses, not even an audience who might be amused. This exchange was only between Andrew, a child of high status, and Germaine, who was completely trusting of the good intentions of others. In this instance I was present and overheard the remark, but I would bet that for every one I heard there were ten I didn't.

That example also illustrates how I have learned to intervene in the interactions of a child like Andrew. Often I see myself as both the guardian of other, less powerful children in the class, and as the reality check for the bad boy's behavior. When a child like Andrew uses his language and influence to hurt or intimidate another child, if I am present, I act as the witness who objects. Because bad boys rely on the co-optation of their co-actors and audience to maintain their status, I see myself as the dissenting voice in the drama.

My early responses when I had first started to see the pattern in the boys' behavior a few years ago had been to simply put the kibosh on it by saying I would not tolerate it in my classroom. That, however, had only served to send the behavior underground, pushing it into spaces like recess, where the children were completely on their own and there was no protection for would-be victims. Gradually I began to change my reaction to what I saw. Instead of suppressing the behavior by forbidding it, I would respond as a co-participant and tell all the players how I was reacting. For example, consider the following exchange between Andrew and Daniel.

ANDREW: Daniel, I know how you got on the Town Soccer Team.
DANIEL: How?
ANDREW: Your father was one of the referees, that's how.

Obviously I overheard those remarks, and my response at that time was completely honest. I asked Andrew if he had made the town team. He replied that he hadn't. I wondered out loud if what he'd just said to Daniel had been said because he felt bad about not making the team and was a bit jealous. Andrew had shrugged and said, as he walked away, "Maybe,

maybe not." Daniel, an easygoing, warm-hearted child, had not said a word in his own defense, but in response to my remarks had smiled at me and rolled his eyes as if to say, "I don't know where that came from."

My intentions in my own participation in these incidents was to call the boys' attention to how their words affected me, because I believe they respected my opinion. Rather than being defiant, as they would have been had I simply banished the exchanges, they become subdued and thoughtful. Sometimes they even apologized privately to the offended child later in the day. Sometimes I think much of what these boys do surprises even themselves. At certain points I have gotten the feeling that they will start a dynamic in motion on an impulse and then find themselves not in control of the event they have orchestrated, and not really liking the outcome or themselves.

As a teacher who has been designated to make the classroom safe for all the children I teach, I view my role as one who responds honestly to a classroom event. If I feel a child's dignity is being affronted, I will say so. If I am feeling offended or hurt on behalf of another child, I'll say so. Sometimes, as other chapters will show, if I am amused by a child's shenanigans, I'll join in on some level. As a teacher researcher, over time I can see the patterns and nuances of the children's performances. With the bad boys, I was able to point out to them what I saw, both to make them aware of the results that I was observing and to begin to have them clarify what they really wanted to have happen socially. Much of my work in this area went on in private, and a look at those kinds of interactions helps us to see the bad boys more completely and to draw connections between the relationship of their private motives and understandings—that is, their subtextual agendas—and their public personae.

DROPPING THE BAD BOY ROLE

It was very cold back when life was hard
Now and then.
They would hear the caribou trot.
What I think is what I think.
A poem is just a thought.
                    —Andrew, *"Poem for the Early Americans," February*

As I pointed out in opening this chapter, the term "bad boy" is a caricature. It is a caricature because it is the way the bad boy operates in the public sphere, when he correctly perceives that he is on stage and is in character. In private interactions these boys are sometimes quite different, especially after they have formed an opinion of my intentions. As a teacher, I felt it was important for me to be able to see these children in other ways, and I made that possible by watching them at all times. Partly I was vigilant with them because of their tendency, as we have seen above, to use public conversations with other children to displace them. But I also was struck by our private encounters, and puzzled by them.

Tony, who we shall see more of later, was a very bad boy. His behavior throughout the school was notorious for its subtle, quiet rejection of authority. In writing about him previously, I said:

> He refuses to participate in group discussions and harasses student teachers, music teachers, art teachers, gym teachers, and substitutes in a number of increasingly subtle ways. He sits in the back of the group, talking softly to his friend, ignoring requests to be quiet, turning his body away from a teacher when he is addressed. (1994, p. 58)

That excerpt later pointed out Tony's other side, a child who loved drawing, performance, and even dance. In February of his second-grade year, I made the following entry in my field notes:

> Tony is in the blocks with Michael this afternoon. He and Michael have been returning regularly to the block corner this week and play variations of "Klingons." Yesterday I heard some strange language in there, almost like baby talk, but I wasn't sure. It was so uncharacteristic. When I went to look, what do I see but a big, blasé, 8-year-old boy, playing blocks with a 6-year-old and talking baby talk.

Charles, whom I cited as a first-grade bad boy when he killed me off in one of his early sharing time stories (1994, pp. 66–67), was a student of history. One day at the end of first grade, when we were staying in from recess on a rainy day, I came upon Charles sitting alone at a small table. As my field notes relate:

> A huge book is opened on the table to a picture of John Brown at Harper's Ferry. It's a reproduction of a painting. John Brown looms in the center, Bible in one hand, rifle in the other. Beneath him are armed men; two lie dead at his feet. The Confederate flag flies in the background, as does the Union flag. Slaves cower in the rear. The sky above is ominous.
>
> Charles has a piece of white paper on the table on which he has sketched the corners of the picture in, copying the borders. I pull over a chair and ask him what he's doing. He explains that he is beginning

a book on "old things," and is going to use the picture. I tell him how Imani had given us that book when she left to move away last December. He smiles, remembering Imani, who used to cuff him on the back of the head when he and Michael were being bad in story and sharing time, but whom he loved dearly. We recall how Charles had come to school on Imani's last day with us in December wearing his Santa Claus suit because she had never seen Santa Claus.

I remark to Charles how I'd noticed his interest in old things, and he agrees, saying that he is really interested in castles and knights, in battles and armor. We converse about this and I realize that what I have previously interpreted to be Charles's callous disregard for the suffering that war and conflict entails is more accurately a fascination with history and times past. From his face, which is smiling and animated as he discusses with me what happened to John Brown, I note that it is so easy to misinterpret the smiles and excitement that this bad little boy shows on his face when he talks about war as glee and pleasure in what is terrible.

"What were things like when you were little, like in the little nickel stores?" he asks naively (obviously placing me, by virtue of being a grownup with grownup children, in the early part of this century). We talk for a while about what that era might have been like. Charles continued to reminisce extensively about the "old times," and things he'd seen from those times. He then went on to recall times in his own past whose memories he clearly relished, and said he was "going to make an old-fashioned place of all of my Legos. I wish the knights and the old-fashioned cars were still around. Like if we were here, and everything around us changed to be knights and castles."

Here, after almost nine months together, was a child I had not seen. Through encounters like these, and in the process of recording them, I realized that I did not always understand how these boys were processing their life in the classroom because I had not distinguished between their public personae and their private selves. Eventually these kinds of interactions helped me to look at these children more carefully and intervene in their public behaviors with knowledge about their private selves and the kinds of experiences they valued.

BAD BOYS AND ADULTS

Children's social actions are almost always within their control. If they are threatening or intimidating others, I believe they know what they are doing.

I also believe that they are hoping for an honest response from everyone present because they are trying on ways of being in the world. The classroom, the playground, and the neighborhood are like experimental test sites for later life. Everyone needs to know the positive and negative effects of what they do. Bad boys, like most children, are not naturally mean spirited; they are experimental. They are small social scientists studying the effects of their behavior on others. The experiments begin at home and gradually expand outward into the world. At all stages of their investigations they need thoughtful "others" helping them to reflect upon and take responsibility for their actions. When I have been able to work with children like Andrew, Charles, Michael, Tony, and Tom for more than a year, their attitude toward power and authority in the classroom begins to alter. This happens, I think, because I am able to spend time making contact with them on a personal level, breaking down the social distance that is required to maintain an attitude of superiority and defiance. And further, they begin to care about the well-being of their classmates. At those points, as a later chapter will show, bad boys begin to change their approach to power, seeing it as something to share with others for the amusement of all.

CHAPTER 4

Silence as a Fortress and a Prison

This chapter is about silence. It is also, like the chapters on bad boys, about power. It describes two years of work that I did following my observations of bad boys. The story begins with a description of the barriers that a 6-year-old girl's silence placed in my way as her teacher, and my efforts to penetrate that silence. It ends with my perception that her silence should also be fiercely guarded. My efforts to work with Rachel represented the second stage in my inquiry into gender and provided a sharply contrasting view of how a position of power is constructed and maintained.

SILENCE AND GENDER

The topic of silence in schools has often been associated with problems of gender and equity in the classroom, and if my experience as a teacher is common, I can see why. I have never seen truly silent boys, with one exception of a child who was severly disturbed. I have seen boys who are quiet and shy, but not silent. On the other hand, I have worked with truly silent girls, and in fact, I was a silent child, so I bring extensive personal experience to this discussion. Some girls are silent for only a few months. They can eventually be coaxed and reassured out of their silence and will participate in the social life of the classroom. But some, like Rachel, are silent for almost a year, and if they have different teachers every year, could potentially be silent throughout their entire education.

Many gender studies have implied that girls, most girls, are "silenced" in the classroom by ineffective teachers and biased curricula. (See the 1993 AAUW report.) They tend to lump girls into one category—all equally disempowered and unequal. And all boys—that is, the culture's seditious favoritism toward all things male—becomes the reason that all girls are disempowered and unequal. I know what I think about that idea: it's simplistic. Yet gender studies have never, to my knowledge, explored *truly* silent girls, although some have self-consciously pondered why they were

45

omitted (Best, 1983). Why not? Is it because we assume that their silence originates only in the classroom, and that therefore, by readjusting a classroom to be gender-neutral, we can put the voice into these girls? Or is it that lack of attention to silent girls occurs simply because they *are* silent— that is, that they are outwardly such good little girls that they are not interesting enough to merit study, or even (as I have found at times), to keep track of?

STUDYING SILENCES

The stupendous reality that is language cannot be understood unless we begin by observing that speech consists, above all, in silences.
—Ortega y Gassett (1957)

For teachers, and perhaps even for researchers, it is so easy to overlook and forget about "good," silent girls. The forgetting, in fact, is what these girls come to rely upon; it is what makes their life in school easier, though at the same time less fruitful. But as philosophers and linguists have pointed out, one cannot consider speech without studying the silences. Thus although the essence of classroom life is formed around talk, the forms and purposes of silences must be documented and explicated.

When I encountered Rachel, I was struck by her silence both because of my own history as a silent girl and because of the difficulties her silence placed in my way as her teacher. As I worked with her over a two-year period, however, the issue of her silence became much more complex. On one hand, I wanted to break it, to pull her out of it so that I could teach her better, but when she finally began to pull out of it, Rachel revealed what was behind the silence, showing me that it concealed not only fear and a desire for personal power, but a richly imaginative private world. I found that I became her accomplice in protecting her silence even as I was asking her to give it up. This chapter and a later one (see Chapter 11) will describe how the layers of Rachel's silence revealed a distinct approach to the world, and further, how a performance based on silence can have a very powerful effect on the dynamics of a classroom.

RACHEL

When she walked into my classroom as a first grader, Rachel appeared to be the perfect little girl: beautiful, healthy, and intelligent, except for one pervasive problem. She was completely silent. All fall, I worked to bring her out: I was gentle, caring, cajoling, reasonable, sensitive, soft spoken, patient; I expanded my wait time from ten seconds to half a minute. The children, even the bad boys, encouraged her, reassured her, spoke more softly, and waited with me. Nothing. Rachel simply would not speak or participate in classroom discussions of any size. She would not respond to teacher or child questions about anything. She would not work cooperatively with any child other than her best friend, Yukiko, also silent, but with a reason—English was her second language. When pressed by me to speak or at least participate, Rachel was absolutely immovable. I decided that I needed to try and record what was happening to see if I could make some sense of it, but even that decision to look more closely at Rachel presented me with immediate problems.

A DATA GAP

First, if you are using talk as one of your primary tools to study children and yourself and you are studying a silent child, you basically have a data gap. For example, on several occasions when I tried taping early morning work time, I would very casually set the tape recorder down on the table where Rachel and Yukiko were drawing and come back later only to find I had a blank tape. This strategy, when used with a table of boys, would result in tapes filled with unusual and complex language samples. These two girls, however, simply didn't talk, except for a few very minimal comments on each other's pictures, or questions about which color marker to choose. Further, in taping class discussions or sharing times, Rachel was never on the tape. I then had to resort completely to field notes, texts Rachel had written, occasional transcripts when I would basically force Rachel to speak to me, and copies of her artwork. Not until my second year with her did I get any sense of what her spoken language was like. Was she inarticulate? Did she have ideas that made sense? Did she understand the main ideas we were working on? What were her interests, dislikes, confusions? Hers was a very hard track to follow.

In early November of 1992, however, as I became more determined to document her persona in the classroom, I obtained snippets of data that helped me begin to think about the issue of her silence. As time passed, I gathered more and more data, and gradually Rachel broke her silence. Time, however, has only increased and complicated my questions and observations. In writing about her, I have decided to work chronologically through my thinking as it has evolved, describing the themes that emerged over time.

SILENCE AS A PROBLEM

To begin, I will describe the dynamics that made Rachel's silence problematic for myself and for the other children using both field notes and
one of the few transcripts I obtained from Rachel in the first year.

Girl's Only Science Talk: November 12

In this talk, from the start, Rachel was extremely resistant. How do I know
that? As soon as the group of seven girls sat down to talk, Rachel began to
move. She was plopped right in the middle of the circle, almost leaning
on me and Yukiko, then rolling away like a top to the back wall until she
was completely outside the group. Her body was turned away from us, and
if she turned toward the girls, her head would be turned away so that she
didn't have to make eye contact. I said directly to her (on tape):

T: And Rachel, this is going to be a small group, so you really will have
    to help us. You can't, we're going to expect everybody to speak, and
    you're going to have to face the children in the group. Can you
    show me that? Right at them, so that they'll know you're talking to
    them. That's the only way they'll know. (I walk away to get a pencil,
    and leave the tape running.)
DIERDRE: Science questions: it's going to be hard. (Rachel laughs nervously.)
MOLLY: Don't think it's so hard. There's thousand of things.
DIERDRE: I know, but those thousands of things are going to be very,
    very hard.
MOLLY: They're all *hard*, Dierdre.
DIERDRE: I know. They're very hard because we weren't even born in
    that time of day. (Rachel continues to roll around, picking at
    microscopic lint on the rug, not speaking. Teacher returns.)
T: Rachel, we can't speak if you're not sitting and looking at us. (She
    settles for a minute, and then I ask her if she has a question.)
RACHEL (in a whisper): Yeah. How did volcanoes begin?
T: Do you want to talk about how volcanoes happen?
RACHEL: How did volcanoes begin? (She uses her hand to sculpt the
    shape of a volcano, with the hand topping off the volcano in a flat,
    sweeping motion.)
T: Ah. That's a different question. How is a volcano made? When you
    do the shape like that, it makes me think that you're thinking,
    "How is it made?" (We review all the questions the girls have
    suggested. Rachel is still moving agitatedly. I mark an X on the floor
    in chalk to give her a firm space to settle on. We decide to talk

about the question "How did things get their names?" Rachel sits
on the X. Later, at the end of the talk in which Rachel has been
silent, continuing to turn and play with specks on the floor, I speak
to her directly.)

T: Rachel, what do you think? Tell us what you think, 'cause we want
to hear from you, too.

RACHEL: What? (She almost seems like she hasn't been there. The
intonation is up, but slightly puzzled.)

T: What do you think about the way words got their names?

RACHEL: Words got their na—uh . . . uh . . . I'm still thinking about it.
Uh . . .

T: Well, just try to help us. We need everybody's help. (Later, I asked
each girl to give me a word they might have needed to say if they
were living millions of years ago. Each girl said something. Then I
asked Rachel.)

T: What do you think, Rachel, what's something you might have
named? (Rachel is moving, almost on her belly on the X.)

RACHEL: I still can't think of it.

T: No, you can tell us something. (Very long silence, perhaps 30
seconds.)

RACHEL (very softly): I don't need to think it. I don't feel like it. (Later, I
asked her again, the same question.)

RACHEL: I'm still thinking.

T: No, you can't be still thinking. You've got to say something.

RACHEL: But I don't know how. (After the science talk, I spoke to Rachel
and asked her why she didn't talk in the talk. She told me she
"didn't want to . . . 'cause I don't feel like it.")

Field Notes: November 16

Rachel and Michael are working together on a math assignment,
weighing classroom objects. Michael takes a turn weighing an object.
It's Rachel's turn and she weighs a toy polar bear. Michael jumps up
and gets something else, brings it over, and puts it on the balance.
Rachel pulls it out and puts her bear back in. They repeat the sequence. Michael comes over and asks for help (he's been told to do
that). When I go over, Rachel is weighing her polar bear again,
hunched over the balance so Michael can't get in. I ask her to take the
bear out. She mumbles something under her breath and crouches
over the bear, putting her hand on top so I can't remove it. I try to lift
her hand, explaining that it's unfair to Michael, but her grip on the
balance is like steel. I have great difficulty moving her hand with any

dignity, and it angers me that such a "nice girl," so feminine and lovely, can be so hard. I explain, trying to control my anger, that she and Michael are working together, and so she needs to let him have a turn. She very slowly and steadily turns her body away from my hands, which are resting on her shoulder. I can feel that her resistance to my control is located in the center of her body. She is literally withdrawing into herself, almost moving into the furniture like a snail moving into its shell. I wonder if she hasn't even closed her ears.

So our struggles continued. I found in group meetings that Rachel absolutely would not give any indication that she was listening to anyone. If someone was talking, she would be playing with a speck on the floor, spinning her body in circles and semicircles, or whispering silently and continuously to Yukiko. I felt compelled to try and break through this wall. It seemed intentional, differing substantially from the random activity of children I have taught in the past with attention problems or emotional issues. When Rachel twirled, I noticed she would periodically glance at me out of the corner of her eye. I would stop discussions and ask her to look at me, to stop moving, to come sit by my feet, to give me some sign that she was engaged and thinking. This generally had a very short-lived effect. Soon she would be twirling and twiddling at my feet, eyes on the floor, body bent in two like a little frog.

Field Notes: Late November

> In a break-off science talk just for girls in which six other nonthreatening girls are speaking together about a question (in effect, we are practicing how to speak in a group), each girl is taking a turn saying one idea about our question. I give Rachel a cue that in six turns we will ask her to say something. I think perhaps she needs time to be mentally prepared, to steel herself, as it were, for this ordeal. When we come to Rachel, she begins to twist and turn, tracing circles on the floor with her hand, gradually turning away from us. We wait, and the girls very softly reassure her that they won't laugh at her or hurt her feelings, that this is a safe place, but she can't speak or make eye contact with any of them or me. We go another round, and this time we wait again for a long time. It is a gentle and tender silence, so clearly without threat, and suddenly she blurts something out so quickly and without any volume that we can't make out what she said, but we are relieved that she tried, and we tell her so. I suppose that's a start.

SILENCE AND POWER

After a few months, I realized that Rachel was doing exactly what the bad boys did, but from a different vantage point. Bad boys typically manipulate language, including both verbal and nonverbal communication, in such a skillful way that they can often gain control of most classroom discussions and instructional activities. Their understanding of the relationship between language and power is sophisticated and extensive, developing more subtlety as they gain more experience in school.

Rachel's silence had a similar effect on my efforts as a teacher and on other children's efforts to work with her: by refusing to communicate with myself and others, she stopped the reciprocity of social discourse. We were getting a very clear and deliberate message that she would not join us, would not respond to my cues to speak, would make us wait forever to hear one sentence or observation, and that she knew I couldn't *make* her speak. While she was not making a bid to control the dynamics of the entire class, she was effectively controlling the dynamics of our relationship with her. She was extremely powerful, and in some ways more powerful than my bad boys. When bad boys are disruptive, teachers can ask them to leave, or discipline them by keeping them in at recess, or send them to talk to the principal, or call their parents in to school. But how can one punish a child *for silence*?

Further, Rachel had a habit of disappearing without being noticed. In fact, sometimes I would look around the group of children at storytime or just before introducing a new activity and realize that she wasn't there, and that I hadn't seen her in quite a while. Her silence on some levels made her almost invisible. Let me illustrate that point by telling what I call the Bathroom Story.

The Bathroom Story

Field Notes: April 15

> Both my intern and I were out of the classroom today. The substitute reports that around noon, Rachel and Yukiko disappeared. She didn't notice for a while, probably about 40 minutes, and when their absence was reported to her, she found Rachel and Yukiko in the bathroom, cleaning the sinks. She identifies Rachel as the mastermind. The incident seems innocuous enough, but had it been Michael, Tom, or Tony, they would have been missed immediately and much more seriously reprimanded.

Field Notes: April 26

> At around 12:30, after story, I move across the room as the children
> settle down to write and find Rachel and Yukiko casually walking
> up the back steps, drying their hands. I realize then that they've not
> been at story. When I ask them where they've been, Yukiko says,
> "Washing our hands." I had given them permission to do that at
> noon, but 30 minutes of water play wasn't what I'd had in mind. I
> reprimand them both fairly sternly, reiterating "rules" and the
> importance of being at story, and I really am annoyed that they've
> missed story again. Rachel doesn't flinch or look away. I am an-
> noyed with myself at overlooking these girls because they are
> sometimes so invisible. At the same time I realize that part of *my*
> way of being in the world relies on slipping by, or slipping away
> when I'm not inclined to be involved in something or want to avoid
> doing something that's unpleasant or threatening.

Yet when we carefully examine the impenetrable silence of this good
little girl, it becomes immediately apparent that Rachel's silence is instruc-
tive in a disturbing way. She magnifies the problems and outcomes of a
closely guarded silence because she shows how powerful silence can be in
interpersonal dynamics and how intricate the construction of an attitude of
silence becomes over time. Initially Rachel provided the absolute contrast
with bad boys in that her manipulation of language pushed the issues of
power and authority *and their connection with language* into the foreground.

On one hand, she was silent, and often it is assumed that little girls
who are silent are helpless and vulnerable. On the other hand, when we
examine the nuances of her silence, we see that it has many layers, and, as
with the bad boys, it is also about power. Where bad boys deftly maneuver their way by skillfully using tone, gesture, and semantics to control
classroom dynamics, Rachel employed very subtle nonverbal devices. That
is, she controlled the flow of spoken ideas by recognizing the mediating
role of talk in the classroom, but not participating in it. Rachel was also
the queen of shrugs, twirls, and other avoidance gestures, and she would
use these communication techniques with differing levels of success. For
example, her gestures, as they're described in the following observations,
were loaded with meaning, but were not always intelligible to others.

Field Notes: February 11

> As I watch her in a creative movement activity I realize that I need
> to film Rachel's nonparticipation. As her small group works on

developing a performance, Rachel characteristically refuses to participate even when begged by the children. Rather, she spends her time turning, leaping, skipping around and around her group without making eye contact, but always keeping her eye on what they were doing.

February 22

During the early morning exercises, when she is reading the daily schedule for the class, Rachel comes to a point where she doesn't know what to do next and falls silent. She shrugs very subtly (not at once noticeable to me), then again, and I realize suddenly that the shrug is very much her utterance for "I don't know what to do."

Rachel has taught me that shrugs, twirls, glances, and hops, even if done for the purposes of *not* making contact, are communications worth studying for their implied meaning. I now see them as the *tone* in her silence. Thus comes my realization that Rachel's shrugs, whispers, and possibly most of her gestures were utterances that while not voiced were "said," and from my point of view should have been responded to in some way, much as I would respond to another child's voiced utterances, or a male child's direct verbal challenges.

SILENCE AS A PRISON

There was, therefore, an early point at which I knew that Rachel's silence was both within and outside of her control. I saw that she used silence for the purposes of realizing some personal power in her relationships, but she was also entrapped by her silence. Note, for example, her behavior in the first science talk excerpt, where her physical resistance to participation is coupled with her statement as to why she did not speak, "but I don't know how."

When I observed Rachel in those few times that she said anything out loud, I recognized from my own childhood the terror behind her breathlessness, the way she blurted out short phrases and looked frantically for a place to hide. Silence as a personal position is a far safer place from which to maintain a sense of control over any situation, but silence is both a fortress and a prison. The threat to Rachel, in my opinion, lay in the public nature of the classroom: at some point each child must be able to stand up and say what he or she thinks. As her teacher, I kept pressing Rachel to take small steps toward that public discourse. I suspect that in Rachel's mind my pressure, however gentle and well intentioned, compromised her pyschological safety.

Now that I reflect on her behavior, framed as it was in a classroom filled with bad boys like Tony, Tom, Michael, and Andrew, boys who scrutinized and judged every statement, *including the teacher's*, why would Rachel want to speak out loud? As Magda Lewis and Roger Simon point out, "Being allowed to speak can be a form of tyranny" (1986, p. 461). The right to speak out loud and be heard, a dynamic that naive observers might place completely within the control of the teacher, in reality resides within the social dynamics of the classroom community. Those dynamics embody the subtextual and consist of undercurrents of status and dominance *among children*, and, as we have seen, are rarely orchestrated solely by the teacher. Only when the teacher studies the development and process of those dynamics can she or he attempt to mediate them in the service of each child's development as a public person.

FINDING A PUBLIC VOICE

Still, in spite of all those factors and much to my surprise, in March of our first year together following an incident at recess, I observed a clear turning point in Rachel's classroom persona. For our class, that incident became the Stuck in the Mud Story.

Field Notes: Rachel and Yukiko Get Stuck in the Mud: March 23:

> Yukiko and Rachel are playing by the baseball diamond in what, after a week of rain, currently resembles a pond of mud. Yukiko wades in and gets stuck up to her boot tops. Rachel wades in to help her and also gets stuck. They are literally cemented in, and no one is around to help. Three boys from our class, Tom, Donald and Ian, come by and debate whether to help them, but none of them wants to wade in. Finally, they make an attempt, but realize that they'll get stuck, too, and back out of the mud. Rachel decides to try and get out, pulls one booted foot out, falls flat on her face and stomach in the mud, gets up, and (as the boys report to me, absolutely awestruck), "She's still smiling, like she's having fun!" Rachel puts her boot back on her foot, manages to get out of the mud, and goes to look for help. The boys wander off. Rachel returns without help and wades back in to rescue Yukiko. This time, she gets really stuck, up to the very top of her boots. Another second-grade girl walks by and wades in to help. She, too, gets stuck. At this point I arrive to

find the three girls stuck firmly in mucky, sandy mud. Rachel is absolutely having the best time. She's laughing and smiling at the predicament. Finally we manage to find the custodians, who rescue the girls, and their boots. A little later, Rachel and Yukiko return to class as we are finishing story, having changed into spare clothes. I ask them to describe their adventure. Rachel, in a loud, clear, and expressive voice, retells the story (with the boys' interjections). She is so animated and articulate that I, and every one else, pay close attention. We are all completely amused by the whole event, and captivated with her energy *and* her voice. It is the first time I and many of the children have ever heard Rachel speak out loud.

Something about this adventure gave Rachel a new public voice. In the days that followed she began to initiate conversations with me and with other children in the class. One day, about a week later, she had a bottle of perfume from home that she was using to terrorize the boys. I note in my journal that "now when she interacts, she is *so* alive: her eyes are wide open and lit up. Her face has a constant half smile on it. She chases those boys with the perfume leading the way. They return again and again to be chased, sort of hanging around her until she notices and then picks up the bottle in a threatening way. She is still very silent, but much more present. Instead of shutting us out, she's almost *prickly with attention and interest.*"

Thus Rachel's movement into the public world of the classroom began. Although I never completely understood how her silence was broken, I had a suspicion that the transition was made precisely because she found an alternative position within the classroom from which to assert her authority. The Mud Incident became notorious in our classroom folklore, resurfacing as a point of admiration and wonder throughout the following year. Rachel attained in that event something of heroic stature, evoking kudos from even the baddest of the boys. The fortuitous Mud Incident had provided her with a bridge to public conversation with her peers and myself, showcasing her natural bravery and adventurousness, traits she could only reveal to us *outside* the confines of the classroom. Rachel had found a way out of her rigid persona, and the bridge that helped her negotiate that path was a story of risk that in many ways crossed a gender line, giving her a different kind of personal power both in her own eyes and in the eyes of her classmates.

About six months later I had an encounter with Rachel's kindergarten teacher that made me realize how far she had moved from her protected and isolated world into our classroom community. That teacher remarked to me, as she left our classroom after visiting for a few minutes, how Rachel seemed "so grown-up. She has so much to say. I don't remember that at all."

"That," I said to her, "is because she never said anything."

I remembered then how Rachel had not spoken for so many months, and it was somewhat shocking to hear her speaking with her friends. But more surprising was the quality of her voice. It mezmerized: it was deep, rich, and mellifluous, like a treasure. Perhaps it was so beautiful because it was so new. Or perhaps it was the life behind the silences that made her words so rich. Because even as Rachel made her entry into our community, she held onto a rich imaginal world, allowing us to see more of it, but never abandoning it for too long. That story, found in a later chapter, reveals more of the "threads of silence that speech is mixed together with" (Merleau-Ponty, 1964, p. 46), and expands our understanding of the interface between the child's strivings for control and autonomy, and the reality of the social world of the classroom.

CHAPTER 5

Posing

Excerpts from Field Notes: May

Tony walks into the classroom early one morning, pauses by the mirror I've placed next to the children's cubbies, scrutinizes his outfit, takes off his baseball hat and shoves it in his cubby, returns to the mirror to push his hair into place, scowls, and walks out of the classroom and into the boys' room. He returns about five minutes later, his hair damp and rearranged carefully in a side part. He picks up his art journal and goes to his usual seat, positioning himself so that anyone entering the room will see him first. As Ellen comes up the stairs, she sees him, smiles broadly, and greets him. He looks up blankly, regards her for an instant, but does not smile. Then he returns to his journal, drawing intently. His left hand just barely touches his hair, smoothing it slightly.

As I call the children to gather for science talks, everyone finds a place in the circle and settles down. Dierdre is sitting at her table writing, as if she hasn't heard the call. I call again, asking her to join us. She looks up, smiles beatifically, picks up her pencil, and then, as the entire class watches, stands up very slowly, slowly arranges her papers and pencil in a stack, picks them up, and walks languidly across the room to put away her materials. We all watch and wait patiently. Dierdre finally arrives at the circle and locates a place her friends have saved for her. She arranges her body as if it were a reclining sculpture, her legs folded to the side, the weight of her body resting on the opposite arm, eyes averted as if contemplating some unseen vision—a beautiful tableaux.

These are two examples of the ways in which some children orchestrate how their peers *see* them. It is a behavior that seems to emerge in second grade after a child realizes that he or she is physically attractive to others, and one I only began to notice after three years of researching gender in my classroom. It is a phenomenon that has consequences in the classroom, both socially and academically, and it most certainly can have a great impact on the way these children decide to position themselves in the world at large.

From my point of view, most children are pretty. But it is also true that some children are simply beautiful. They have a physical gift that seems to increase as they grow. It is also true that this culture venerates physical beauty, just as it does physical prowess in different forms. The pursuit of beauty is a pervasive quest, primarily for women, but increasingly for men as well. Enormous amounts of money are spent each day as we seek to change or enhance our physical traits in search of the label of "beautiful." We also take pleasure in seeing beautiful people on television, in the movies, in magazines, and as our newscasters.

For some children who are beautiful, the realization of that fact begins in school and is triggered by the behavior of other children. The dawning of the perception in a child that his or her physical self causes other children to act in certain ways can change how she or he behaves in the classroom. The consciousness of being beautiful sets in motion a performance that explores and is intended to maintain the attention of others. In essence, the fact of being beautiful is transformed into a desire to be a thing of beauty. I am proposing that the beautiful child makes him or herself into an object well before other children apprehend how to do that. The making of a "sex object," if you will (because I think that that is what the notion of beauty finally becomes in our culture), from my observations begins with the active "trying on" of the beautiful persona. It begins with posing.

TRYING ON THE BEAUTIFUL PERSONA

What does that mean, psychologically and behaviorally? For the beautiful child, there is first the perception that others are affected by her physical self. That perception, once it is fully apprehended, is followed by a scrutiny of how she affects others, under what circumstances, and in what ways. Essentially, the child begins to try on the persona. Of course, all of this thinking, watching, analyzing, and trying on is occurring in the classroom while she is trying to learn, or on the playground when she is playing with her friends. In effect, her attention, most especially in the classroom, becomes divided.

To put it another way, we could say that the child's intellectual energy or focus becomes compromised by the social, by the subtextual, and finally, by the performance. The child is both inside and outside her body, watching others as they watch her. At the same time, for the other children who are watching her, the intial attraction to a beautiful person is, I believe, an aesthetic one. Other children want to be around a beautiful child simply because he or she is beautiful; they are naturally attracted to beauty and find it compelling both as a point of wonder and as a point of curiosity.

This quite natural response stimulates in the beautiful child the beginning of the cycle of becoming an object: she notices and becomes at first self-conscious, then consciously aware of the state of being beautiful. The first response is one of bewilderment and some confusion about the origins of the attention that she is receiving. The second is a more deliberate awareness that results in different physical and behavioral performances, or poses, similar to those that introduced this chapter. We can think of them as a series of experiments with the social dynamics that physical beauty has set in motion.

DIERDRE

Thus it was with Dierdre. She was physically the perfect prototype of popular culture's notion of beauty. She was tan and slender, with large brown eyes and honey-colored hair. She was also very smart, and popular with the other girls as a friend. Boys, especially second- and third-grade boys, clearly thought she was beautiful and were slightly intimidated by her. I often observed that they became tongue tied if they thought she was listening to them talk, even though she herself was very soft spoken and as a first grader was completely oblivious to their dilemma.

Dierdre realized about two months into her first-grade year that something was up. She wasn't sure what was happening, she told me, but lots of people were "bothering" her on the playground at recess, and she didn't like it. When I inquired about who the "lots of people" were, she mentioned many of the older boys and a few older girls, but it was clear to me she truly did not understand why they were bothering her. She complained about the chasing and grabbing of the second-grade boys but eventually found protection within a coterie of first-grade girlfriends, most of whom rejected the notion of playing with boys and took pains to avoid those contacts. That entire year Dierdre was puzzled by the unsolicited attention but seemed to accept it as a part of playground life.

When she entered second grade, however, something had changed. She was still quiet and soft spoken, but there was a new knowledge in her eyes when she interacted with the boys. She was coy—not necessarily inviting attention, but when it was offered (usually in an aggressive way), she responded with a slight challenge of her own. On the playground it looked something like this: a boy would chase Dierdre and taunt her, hoping she'd chase him. She would simply continue walking or playing with her friends, but would casually reply, "Why would I want to?" The tone was not perjorative, meaning "Why in the world would I want to chase you?" but rather was inviting, meaning, "Give me a few good reasons, and I might."

As I watched Dierdre that second year in the classroom, I noticed that almost all children of any age and background wanted her attention. When the class gathered for story or sharing, or arranged themselves for a discussion, there was considerable vying among the girls for the seat next to her. In the midst of all this, Dierdre seemed not to notice that girls were shoving and pushing each other rather rudely in an effort to sit close to her. If Dierdre was distracted and not listening to whomever was speaking (including myself or another teacher), other children around her would become similarly distracted. If she seemed enthusiastic about an activity, her friends would be the same. One day when I asked Rachel, one of her best friends, who made her feel self-conscious in the classroom, she named all of the bad boys, *and Dierdre*. In spite of my surprise, I realized that Rachel, like all the other children, was in awe of Dierdre and was very conscious of what she might be thinking.

As time went on, I also noticed that Dierdre was the only girl in the class who exchanged verbal quips and challenges with the powerful boys. However, that exchange never occurred in the context of a class discussion or an instructional activity, because by second grade Dierdre no longer participated actively in those events. That in itself was disturbing to me because the change from her first grade behavior was so marked. She had, in effect, ceased to talk about what she thought, had stopped asking questions and proposing ideas. When I observed her in group meetings, I saw that Dierdre's body posture had also altered in second grade. She was no longer unaware of how she looked to others. What I saw was a posture, an almost rehearsed arrangement of her physical self, and it was almost always accompanied by a mannequinesque element that concealed any sign of inner thoughts. In other words, Dierdre knew that other children watched her, and she planned how they would see her. In some cases she even seemed to orchestrate an impression that she was nothing more than her physical presence, as the following field notes reveal.

Sharing Time: November 18

> Dierdre gets in the chair with a large plastic shopping bag and pulls out a box. "I got this for a birthday present. Michael gave it to me last year. I never even opened the box." She begins to undo the plastic

covering. "Hm, I wonder what this is," she says. She pulls the box open, and then continues, "I don't even know what any of this is." (What, I wonder, does Michael think of this?) It seems as if Dierdre wants to know nothing in front of the group: playing dumb! Could that be possible? What's going on here? The children seem to be as puzzled as I am, because she has nothing to tell or show them, and she's acting as if she doesn't care, just peering into the box and wondering out loud what everything is. So no exchange is happening, except that (of course) now I see the boys in the front row are trying to take control (to help her?), and things begin to disintegrate as they grab for objects in the box to see them. No one asks or comments. Dierdre is definitely miffed, and packs up the box, sitting down in the group without looking at anyone. Then, in the next child's sharing, she starts to lounge, basically assuming a posture that implies she couldn't care less about what's going on.

The change from first grade was striking, and it was made more vivid by the fact that I knew Dierdre had a deep interest in learning and study. While her posing gave the impression that she was detached from what was going on, my private interactions with her revealed that she was very interested in what I and her fellow students had to say. Essentially she wanted to be fully with us but did not want to show it; the gaze of others was far too strong to ignore. So Dierdre found herself playing the role of the beautiful girl. That role was both gratifying, because of the attention it drew, and constraining. True, other children always wanted to be with her during all parts of the day, but their attention, and especially the attention of the boys, was distracting to her. It was almost as if Dierdre was disembodied, standing outside herself, watching other children watch her.

Dierdre and Bad Boys

I've noticed in my observations of bad boys at work that they will often use a beautiful little girl as their target. Why they do this is open to speculation. I often think it's because the beautiful little girl is usually very popular and very influential as a social operator. Beauty in women and men in our culture is obviously worth a lot of currency. It's no different for children. Beautiful children are sought after as friends simply because of their beauty. And young boys are attracted to beautiful girls, but they're also intimidated by them. From my experience, this attraction produces behavioral changes in most young boys as soon as they start school. Beauty, however, as we will soon see, works both for and against you, even when you're only seven years old. In the mind of a boy who is interested in power, we could say that he both wants the attention and admiration of the beautiful little girl and wants to control her so that she doesn't take too much of it away from him.

One morning, Andrew got in the chair to share and said he was going to tell a fake story, something he often did and did well. He sat down, made himself comfortable, and began a story about how he and all the other boys in the class were walking across a desert and came to a river of ice cream. The boys nodded and licked their lips with approval. Andrew continued:

> I took out my straw and started to sip, but the straw got plugged up. And when I took the straw out to look at it and see what was wrong, I saw a tiny Dierdre stuck in it.

The boys' and girls' eyes widened and they oohed and aahed.

> Then, I took Dierdre home in the straw and put her in the microwave on full power.

"Yikes!" exclaimed the girls.

"Right on," called out a few boys. Dierdre was silent and still, her face a mask. Andrew went on:

> And then I was tired, so I fell asleep for twelve hours, and the microwave was on full power. The next morning I woke up and looked in, and there was Dierdre, fried, and covered with plastic.

Andrew did an impression of the now fried Dierdre, flattening himself against the chair, his legs and arms spread eagled, his eyes frozen wide open, his face a frozen scream.

"Oh, no!" exclaimed the girls, clapping their hands over their mouths.

"Yes!" called out the same few boys. Dierdre remained motionless.

Andrew went on to describe how he took Dierdre back to the Ice Cream River and put her back in. But then she was washed out to sea, and when she tried to get out of the ocean, she "landed on a shore of quicksand, and was sucked into an ant nest. Only it was Fire Ants!"

At that point Andrew's time to share ran out, and a few boys asked for more details of the ant hill, but the girls did not ask any questions. Dierdre still had not moved or spoken, and she showed no emotion. I raised my hand and Andrew called on me. I said I had a question for Dierdre and asked her if she had minded Andrew's story. She turned toward me and shrugged, her face tight lipped and pale.

"It's okay," she said softly, and tried to smile. However, I knew that it hadn't been okay for me, and I told Andrew it had scared me and I didn't want to hear stories like that, which hurt someone I cared about. The other girls nodded in agreement, and a few added that they didn't like it when the girls were "beaten up" in some boys' stories, but Dierdre was still silent. Andrew sat down next to his friends without comment.

Dierdre and Other Children

This was certainly not the only time that Dierdre figured centrally in a story by a bad boy. It is interesting, however, that it was only the bad boys who put her in a story with a menacing plot. All the other children included her in their stories as a normal participant. But she was *always* in the other stories, whereas not every other child was. One could see her constant inclusion in the other children's imaginary stories as carrying a very subtle message for Dierdre. There was the implicit message that they all admired her, but there was also the sense that she constantly figured in their awareness, that they were always noticing her.

If I were to describe what Dierdre's place was in the social hierarchy of the classroom, I would probably use the common term from my childhood that is still used to describe children, especially girls, who receive a lot of attention from their peers. We could say that Dierdre was very "popular." When I hear that term used to describe children, the implicit meanings of the word "popular" are never examined. Popular children are those who, for reasons usually attributed to their clothes or their looks, are sought after as friends. Often the essence of the popularity is dismissed by adults, and later by peers, as something superficial and without real substance. Often the word is used pejoratively, to imply that the child in question is shallow or lacks other gifts. That, however, is not a useful characterization for anyone who works with, cares about, or is raising children.

Dierdre *was* popular. It had nothing to do with her clothes or material goods. In fact she rarely called attention to herself with clothing. It was the result of other children's natural desire to be with her because they were physically attracted to her. But in some way the attention she got made her less able to be herself in school. She often denied herself the right to speak freely about her thoughts, to ask questions in front of her friends, to be completely goofy and childlike. Being beautiful, being popular, was time consuming, and as we've seen from Andrew's story, sometimes risky, at least on a metaphoric and symbolic level.

BEAUTIFUL BOYS

Although I've described the plight of the beautiful child from close observation of a girl, I want to point out that beautiful boys often suffer the same dilemmas. And further, some beautiful boys are also bad boys.

The detachment required for both roles seems to mesh well, adding more power to those boys' performances. In fact, bad boys who are also physically beautiful have the most dominance in a class and sometimes even in a school. In my experience, the dynamics described earlier of Dierdre's adoption of the beautiful persona also occurs for beautiful boys like Tony. The initial reactions of other children, the growing awareness of their attention, the posing, the performance, the withdrawal from classroom participation, the suppression of their thinking in public, and the pursuit by other children of both the same and opposite sex happens for boys.

When Tony was a first grader, he went through many of the same experiences that Dierdre had upon entering first grade. He was chased by girls, especially second-grade girls, and as the year progressed it became clear that he was aware of the effect he had on others. He carefully cultivated a detached attitude in class, rarely contributing to discussions or speaking in front of the class. By second grade, as he moved into a very dominant role in the classroom, he was constantly trailed and openly admired by Charles, Andrew, and Michael, who were first graders, and it was clear from the children's sharing time stories that Tony was on everybody's mind. Like Dierdre, Tony was always a central figure in fake stories. In fact, for most of his second-grade year, Tony was included in a fake story at least once a day by both girls and boys.

The nature of the stories, however, was different. Usually Tony was a humorous and powerful central figure. His character lived in a mansion, had silver chairs and tables and magical tools, but was aloof and detached from the more mundane struggles of his friends. Here is a typical excerpt from a story:

> Tom and Ian were still in jail, and they found Tony's magic marker and they kept drawing things: a bed, covers, a larger room. And then they drew themselves right out of the jail, and they came up under Tony's silver chair and broke it. Tony was in his room waiting to get his money for the expensive silver toilet Tom had broken the last time he dug out of jail, so he added the cost of the chair to the toilet.

Sometimes, however, being a central figure, although not dangerous metaphorically, could be risky. The boys, in telling a round robin story one day, placed Tony in a bar with Madonna. Here is Charles's turn:

> Then I saw Michael, and he said, "Will you go to the bar? And we went to the bar and saw Tony and Madonna. And they were, you know, "Ooh-la-la!", and all the people went, "Whoo, whoo!"

And Michael continued:

> And there were, like, tons of Madonnas standing on the bar counter, and tons of little Madonnas running around and flying around the bar. And Tony drank oil, and there was a fire, and he forgot that he drunk oil, and the fire got bigger.

And Donald:

> And so Tony went to get a taxi, and, oh no! The taxi driver was Madonna. Ahh. And Tony went home and was going to tell his Mom, but oh, help, *he was Madonna!*

This story, while not as violent as the one Andrew told about Dierdre, was also sexually suggestive and placed Tony in a compromising situation. It also required him to sit by and listen mutely as his friends placed his character in ever more risky situations. Like Dierdre, Tony would never object to being included in anyone's story, but he rarely showed pleasure at being included, and his presence in so many stories signaled to him that the children were watching him, and, in a way, desiring him. It was a condition that he had cultivated, and it was also confining and silenced him in different ways.

For Tony, posing set him up to be a powerful presence in the class. He was a bad boy, and he was beautiful. Unlike bad boys who were not physically beautiful, Tony had the added burden of maintaining the pose at all times. Increasingly in second grade, he would not allow himself to be completely childlike or silly. That kind of spontaneity became less and less comfortable for him as a way to interact with his classmates, and his public persona was without extreme emotions of any kind. Tony was always extremely composed, both emotionally and physically. He never allowed himself to show pain, sadness, joy, or anger, or to ask a question or admit that he didn't understand something.

For both Tony and Dierdre, the assumption of the posing role constrained them as it became more and more rigid. By the end of second grade, both of these children, thoughtful, quiet, and sensitive, did not allow themselves to make real childlike contact with their friends, or with me. Once again the social status that the role conferred on them, and the authority it gave them over other children, was too compelling to abandon.

CHAPTER 6

The Saturday Game

Tony: Saturday.

Donald: Tony, come on, stop it.

Tony: Don't you know Saturday, Monday?

Donald: Tony. You know, there was this movie? There's this guy. His name is Crocodile Dundee.

Tony: No, but was it on Saturday?

Donald: Yes, I did watch it Saturday.

Tony (with a deep breath): Then. Everything's called Saturday, so his name isn't, whatever, his name is Saturday. You have to say everything Saturday.

Thus, on March 12, a Monday, began a language game based on a rule that improvised on the word "Saturday." This wordplay gradually permeated much of these boys' private exchanges and eventually percolated into many whole class discussions which the central powerful boys, who had made the rules, orchestrated. Following the development of the game gives me a chance to present bad boys in another light. Perhaps it will help the reader see them as children who, in their second year with their classmates and their teacher, started to use their skill at language to entertain and influence the class in different ways, ways that reflected a growing interest in becoming part of the community rather than working against it.

When Tony walked into the classroom that Monday morning, he began a game with his friend, Donald, that was not unusual. I had observed and audiotaped bad boys playing similar word games with only their friends for two years in my classroom. I had also observed my son and his teenaged friends casually playing in similar ways with both changes in word meanings and with different street dialects in our living room, when they'd thought I was out of earshot. When I happened to catch the beginning of the "Saturday" exchange on tape, I found it fascinating, but I had no plans to track it further. It was not until it began to turn up in other conversations, causing both consternation and amusement among other children in the class, that I took a closer look. [The original and later word usage in this game is similar to what the Opies (1959) call "tangletalk," as they documented it in their work in the British Isles. Tangletalk is defined as "the deliberate juxtaposition of incongruities" in children's ditties and rhymes (p. 24).] While the Opies describe tangletalk in Britain as improvisations on known rhymes from folklore, the Saturday game was a pure improvisation on the word "Saturday."

TONY: But Donald, do you know what Saturday is?
DONALD: Yes, Saturday is Saturday and everything on Saturday is Saturday. So here, I'll tell you something that I did on Saturday. I Saturday'd on Saturday, Saturday is Saturday. And I Saturday'd . . .
TONY: Do you know what Sunday is? Sunday? Sunday is Sunday.
DONALD: Isn't that nice? And I Sunday'd . . . on Sunday, I Sunday'd and on Sunday, I Sunday'd. And I Sunday'd on Sunday. On Sunday, I Sunday.
TONY: Donald, is it Saturday, Saturday?
DONALD: Oh, Saturday, Saturday.
TONY: Monday.
DONALD: Monday, I Monday'd. On Saturday, I Saturday'd.
TONY: No, on Saturday, you *be* Saturday.
DONALD: On Saturday, I *be* Saturday.
TONY: No, you don't be Saturday.
DONALD: On Saturday, I *don't* be Saturday.
TONY: Then you *be* Saturday.
DONALD: On Saturday, I be Saturday.
TONY: And then you be Thursday, on Saturday, on Friday, on Saturday.
DONALD: On Saturday, I'm Thursday.
TONY: Nope, on Thursday, on Saturday. On Saturday, on Friday.

At first, as Tony and Donald played, Donald took the role of following Tony's leads. He reluctantly went along with Tony in the beginning, wanting at first to tell Tony the story of Crocodile Dundee. But Tony, who was the more dominant child, pushed the Saturday game, and soon Donald was enthusiastically improvising, changing Saturday from a noun to a verb. Then Tony threw out the line: "On Saturday, you *be* Saturday" and Donald made that change, beginning a new volley of improvisations.

It is interesting to note that the shift Tony directed here to using the naked "be" as part of the game began a sequence that reflects what Smitherman (1986) and others have characterized as one of the rhetorical qualities of black discourse. By changing the use of the word to a verb of being, Tony altered the meaning of the game and Donald easily made the shift. A bit later in the game, the voice shifted even more and took on a rhythmic jive quality that is clearly a result of the influence of black English on mainstream culture: "Take out you eyeballs. Crack you head open. Smack me with a board. Just do a bad thing on Saturday." It is important to point out here that bad boys and their close friends are the only young non–African American children I have ever heard making that dialiect shift into black English. That kind of language is often a part of their private talk and wordplay but rarely, if ever, surfaces in more formal classroom conversations.

At that point their friend Tom sat down at the table and there was a pause in the game, but the boys soon moved on to grossing each other out, and adding a slight change in dialect and rhythm:

DONALD: No, I'm laughing at you on Saturday.

TONY: No, you're supposed ta' pour saliva on Saturday.

DONALD: No, I gonna barf on you Saturday.

TONY: Why are you doing all that stuff on Saturday because you're only supposed to do Saturday stuff?

DONALD: I know Saturday stuff is . . .

TONY: Take out you eyeballs, crack you head open. Smack me with a board. Just do a bad thing on Saturday.

DONALD: Why bad things on Saturday?

TONY: Because it's 1981, five hundred eighty-one. You can do whatever you want because on next Saturday, at one in the morning, the country's gonna blow up. So you can do whatever you want. Have as much gambling, you can. Give away your money, it doesn't matter. Just do what you want Saturday. Is that all?

DONALD: I'm telling.

TONY: It *is* on Saturday.

DONALD (leans over Tony and addresses Tom, who had been sitting quietly next to Tony): Tom, do you believe the world's going to blow up on Saturday? Do you believe it?

TOM: Uh-huh. It says so on the news.

DONALD: No one knows if it is.

TONY: Yes, scientists think. It's going to blow up.

TOM: No, next Saturday.

TONY: Next Saturday.

DONALD: Okay. It will be the Saturday after next.

TONY: Next Saturday, eighteen fifty-five. Isn't it, Tom? (Silence.) Uh-huh . . . uh-huh . . . yes sirree. It's going to blow up. You can ask my dad.

So at this point the original players included three boys: Tony, Donald, and Tom. Although Tom had arrived late, he was carefully listening to the exchange as he drew. In the events of the next few weeks, it was clear that he understood the game.

SATURDAY RESURFACES

On Wednesday, March 17, as Tom was reading the day's schedule to the class and writing the date on the calendar, Donald said under his breath, "It's Saturday." I was sitting in the back of the group on the floor close to Donald and Tony, who usually sat next to each other with their backs against the wall, and heard Donald's remark. Apparently several other children did, too. They turned to him and protested, "No, it's Wednesday!"

"Saturday," said Donald, without moving, smiling, or changing the deadpan expression on his face. Tom glanced at Donald, smiled, and finished writing the date. The other children continued to grumble in annoyance, throwing puzzled looks toward Donald.

"Every day is Saturday," added Tony softly. Tony and Donald smiled slyly, not making eye contact.

"Saturday" did not surface again in the classroom, at least to my knowledge, until April 12. I was not sure how far it had spread among the inner circle of boys during that time. Tony walked into the room at 8:20 A.M., went directly over to two second-grade girls, Ellen and Molly, and Dierdre, then a first grader, who were drawing together, and said, "It's Saturday." The girls stopped drawing and looked up absentmindedly.

MOLLY: Yeah.
ELLEN: What do you mean? It's not Saturday, it's Tuesday.
TONY: No, it's Saturday. Every day is Saturday. *Your name* is Saturday.

The girls disagreed loudly with him and asked him again what he meant. Tony smiled, shrugged, and walked away. They continued to talk among themselves, playing with it a little bit, but then losing interest.

MOLLY: If yesterday is Saturday and today is Saturday, and tomorrow is
    Saturday, then every day is gonna be Saturday.
ELLEN: Do you get it?
MOLLY: No.
ELLEN: I don't get it. I don't get the point.
DIERDRE: I don't get the point, either. He didn't really tell us why it's
    Saturday.

Silence fell again as the girls seemed to lose interest, but then Donald, who was sitting at a nearby table, chimed in.

DONALD: I know why it's Saturday! Because . . . it's Saturday!
ELLEN: Then why are we in school?
DONALD: Because it's Saturday!
(At this point Charles and Michael, then first graders, tried to join in.)
CHARLES: We're imagining!
DONALD: No, *we're* not. It *is* Saturday.
MICHAEL: We're imagining we're in school!
ELLEN: I just pinched myself to make sure I was awake, and I was awake!

Now the discussion was attracting attention from many children, like the two first-grade boys who did not really know what was going on. Donald responded to Ellen's last remark: "No, you're just *thinking*! You're not asleep, you're just *thinking*!"

From far away across the room, I could hear Tony exclaiming to himself: "Saturday! Today is Saturday!" Then he turned to Yukiko, who was walking by his table, "You're Saturday." She shrugged, smiled, and walked on.

At this point, Tony and Donald were both still clearly in charge of this event, but seemed to want to bring it into the mainstream of classroom talk, almost inviting the girls to try to participate. As I observed, I felt that Tony's remark to the girls seemed to have been a deliberate act to make the game public and cause a sensation. Donald was also sitting suspiciously close to the girls that morning. Although children in my classroom do not have assigned seats, their morning journal places are predictable. The girls usually sat in a particular spot, as did Tony and Donald, and those places were rarely close together—so it seemed to me that Tony and Donald had planned this particular incident. I was especially fascinated by who they chose to try the Saturday game out on: Ellen and Molly were very dominant girls in the classroom community, known both for their intelligence and for their bravado on the playground with the boys, while Dierdre, who we met in Chapter 5, was an object of attention for all the children. These girls regularly played with the boys, wrestling, chasing, and tumbling with the best of them. Molly, who had a reputation in the class as a sort of language maven, did in fact try to play briefly with the "Saturday" riddle.

After Ellen remarked that she had "pinched" herself and "was awake," Donald's reply almost seemed like he was coaching her: "No, you're just *thinking*! You're not asleep, you're just *thinking*!" In other words, "Stop thinking, and play." At all times, the boys used a ringing, sonorous tone, as if they were performing for the other children, who could clearly overhear them. But when, in characteristic fashion, Charles and Michael, who seriously emulated Tony and Donald as role models, tried to join in,

Donald's response clearly indicated that they were not yet part of the game. His tone of response to Charles' assertion "We're imagining" was dismissive: "No, *we're* not. It *is* Saturday." Donald was not calling simply for imagination; he was calling for performance, and he did not see the performance as automatically open to uninvited players. In this case, the players had to figure out the rules to be part of the "Saturday" game.

At this point, I called the class to the meeting area to begin the day, and after opening exercises, we shared our art journals. I had continued to carry my tape recorder and was audiotaping when Tom began the following narrative.

Tom (showing his picture): This is the inside of me. I was trying to have
    a parade of firecrackers. Instead I blew my bottom off. Ellen's
    smoking dynamite (pointing to the figure in the picture). Tony
    drew Ellen like this, but without the dynamite.
Ellen: Why do you always make it be me?
Tom: Cause you're the only one we can gross out. (Ellen smiles.)

Then, without thinking, I raised my hand and Tom called on me.

Teacher: Did you draw this on Saturday?
Tom (startled, he pauses for several seconds): Yeah, every day is Satur-
    day. Except Thursday, cause that's the Simpsons and we can't miss
    The Simpsons.

Tom continued with the following narrative, which I've broken up to represent his chantlike phrasing.

> Monday got the chicken pox.
> Tuesday got the heebie-jeebies.
> Boogie, boogie, boogie, boogie.
> Wednesday died
> And Friday got pneumonia.
> Everyday is Saturday.

Saturday chants broke out among all the boys. The girls sat quietly, smiling and shrugging. Molly rolled her eyes. Then both Donald and Tony asked to add in their own versions of the Saturday story. The class listened politely, but did not respond. After that meeting, the "Saturday" game seemed to go back underground. However, occasionally in response to another child's sharing of a picture or an object, someone would ask if it had been made "on Saturday," provoking groans, protests, laughter, and the rolling of eyes among everyone in the class. It had become a class joke, thrown in whenever the discussion seemed to warrant it.

Because I had been a witness to the beginning of the game, I knew the inside joke and could follow its progress. When I asked the question of Tom, it just sort of popped out. In fact, I think unconsciously, I really wanted to play the insider game and asked the question for my own amusement, much as Tony or Donald might have asked the same question. There is in this kind of game an edge of humor and theatre which, if one understands the rules, can be quite funny; and when the boys finally began to play in public, there was also an overture of camaraderie with the rest of the class that was unusual, especially for Tony and Tom.

From my experience observing powerful boys, this kind of language play is not at all unusual in their private exchanges. What was unusual was their decision to introduce it into the public discourse, thus making the game one everyone could enjoy. Tom had always specialized in a kind of wisecracking language that very few children, except his male friends, could follow or understand. As we have seen in previous chapters, Tony was usually a quiet, taciturn, and very powerful bad boy who rarely even acknowledged the presence of children he did not consider to be worthy of his attention. This game, however, which clearly started as one of the boys' private exchanges, moved into the mainstream of the language community of our classroom, allowing everyone to play on some level. How that movement occurred is hard to determine. Part of it might have come from Donald's influence.

A LOOK AT A GOOD BOY

Donald, in spite of his close friendship with two bad boys, was a very good boy. He was quiet, respectful, serious, and cooperative, and he really enjoyed being a student and being taught. Authority was not an issue for him. He took most people quite seriously, and although he had a mischevous side, it never threatened other children. Donald also had a performative side that I first saw in the end of his first-grade year with me when he took to singing our favorite class songs in a psuedo-operatic tone, much to the delight of his very bad friends, who immediately adopted the style. In fact, that trend continued into second grade, when it was taken up with gusto by every boy in the class. Our end of the day sing-alongs would become spectacular, full-voiced, puffed-up, vibrato-laden, operatic renditions of simple children's songs like "Five Green Speckled Frogs" or "Down by the Bay." Any other adults present would be absolutely bowled over by the performances of these macho, callous boys turned opera divas.

Donald was clearly not a bad boy, but he was admired and sought after by bad boys as a friend. His position in the class was based not on brokering authority by manipulating others through the subtle use of language, but by treating others with respect and using words to amuse all of us. When his friends were working other children over, he would not object, but neither would he participate. He almost seemed to fade into the background, even though he was often sitting next to the bad boys. Yet he was also supremely aware of the subtleties of language, using his skills masterfully to quietly entertain teachers, with humorous asides about our work, and children, with an endless stream of fake stories about a character, himself, who had a great deal of trouble counting. This character would spend the duration of each fake story trying to dig his way out of a prison with a plastic spoon. He would dig slowly and meticulously, counting every spoonful of dirt, then become distracted by another event or thought and lose count at ninety-nine, at which point he would start the process over again. As a result, week after week the character never made any progress, but Donald's variations on the digging never got old. He had a supremely subtle feel for the language of humor and understatement, and he used only himself as the foil for his humor.

His fake stories were immediately adopted as part of the canon of stories told in the classroom, and Donald happily let anyone use the plastic spoon and counting gimmick for any new purpose. His influence on the class's shared stories extended quietly in many directions. At one point after I'd referred to "an albatross around my neck," Donald asked where that reference came from, and after I told him and gave him a brief synopsis of the "The Rime of the Ancient Mariner," he requested a class reading of the poem. That reading, done at storytime with the whole class of first and second graders, took well over three weeks and was met with fascination by all the children. Donald followed that event with a series of portraits of "Death" in his art journal, portraits he drew each morning for over a year with accompanying captions that rendered the macabre drawings funny: "Madonna Death," "Boar's Head Death," "Great White Death." Soon his friends and other children were also drawing their own renditions of Death and weaving stories around them.

In his own quiet way, he was extremely influential in the classroom, but not in a manner that usurped any other child's personal authority. It was most likely Donald who moved the Saturday game into the mainstream of classroom life, orchestrating with Tony a performance that precipitated that movement.

THE POWER OF COMMUNITY

In my earliest writings on bad boys, I stated my hope that:

> as they see that school is not a battleground . . . they will begin to alter their
> own personal picture of where their personal power lies. In the end, I want
> these boys to experience how powerful it is to belong and fully commit one-
> self to the creation of a dynamic learning community where, rather than strug-
> gling continuously to assert their superiority and control, they work to fuel
> the intensity and excitement of everyone's participation. (1994, p. 70)

It has become clear to me that indeed, this movement into community
life can happen for these boys, and that it can markedly alter their goals as
power brokers while also positively changing the social climate of the class
as a whole. That was the case for Tony, Tom, and Donald. But this kind of
alteration cannot be counted on. It relies, rather, on the particular chemistry of a social group. If we consider the nature of performance, we know
that each player contributes to the quality, intensity, and aesthetics of the
performance—and that, in turn, influences the audience's reaction and the
impact of the performance on their lives.

In this case, Donald played a vital role in changing his friends' use of
language from one of control to one of participation and audience involve-
ment. He successfully introduced the bad boys to the different kind of social
action he practiced, and that work on his part helped them to diversify
their roles. In some cases, as we shall see in the following chapters, when
children's social objectives do not mesh, completely different results can
occur. We will watch as certain children try to influence the thinking of
the whole class, and uncover the ways in which the subtextual dynamics
of particular children, when brought into full view, influenced all the players, but with outcomes very different from those elicited by the Saturday
Game.

CHAPTER 7

Your Mother Squeezes Your Brains Out Your Ears

It is a sunny April afternoon and I am out on the playground, watching the children play. As I stroll around its edges, I notice Ellen half-sitting, half-reclining on the grass. Molly and Amy jump rope close by on the blacktop. Tony, Donald, Tom, and Ian walk over to Ellen. They stop, and Tony bends over and begins to speak to her. Molly and Amy stop jumping rope, turn to look at the boys, and then move away from the area. Ellen remains, still reclining. The boys hover over her. As I come closer, I hear Tony say, almost in a whisper, "Your mother squeezes your brains out your ears."

I recognized this as the kind of talk Ellen had complained about recently in class. At that time, Tony had followed Ellen around the classroom, speaking in very low tones. As he passed by me, I heard him say, "Then he'll take your guts and rip them out, and blood will come out of your ears." It was graphic blood-and-guts talk, and it was very pointedly directed at her. When she complained to me, I told him to stay away from her because he was disturbing her, and he complied without protest.

I didn't pay much attention to that incident until I observed the second. Then, when I realized what Tony and the boys were doing, I was annoyed. At first glance, Ellen looked like she was plastered to the ground—one might almost say, cowering. Then, as I watched her friends who could overhear the remarks move away, I wondered why she stayed. I also saw that the three other boys were watching, but not talking to Ellen. Donald, though, was hovering over her, almost seeming to contain her with his body as Tony whispered. Ian and Tom were on the side, watching and looking very serious. There were no smiles; no one was laughing and joking as they would have done with each other. It seemed very ominous.

When I heard what Tony was saying, I stopped and told all the boys that I thought that kind of talk should not be used with other children. I knew they enjoyed talking that way with each other, but I didn't think Ellen liked it. The boys shrugged and drifted away. After I spoke to the boys, Ellen got up and left, but not until I had asked, "Ellen, does that talk bother you?"

"I don't know," she said, "I'm not sure."

"I DON'T KNOW, I'M NOT SURE"

A hallmark of Ellen's persona in school was that she never prejudged people or ideas. When I reflect on the incident and on my approach to it, her attitude seems now to be a gift of special intelligence. Ellen never accepted something as true because her mother or father or I said it was true. She always asked why, or, "How do you know?" She always wanted to explore something before she stated her own opinion of it. Here was a case where Ellen's ambivalence made me rethink what I was seeing. I had assumed (as would most teachers who knew Tony and Tom) that the boys' motives were less than honorable. After all, they were very bad boys, and as we saw earlier, wordplay was their forte, any category was fair game, and the game was often used to intimidate others. But Ellen's response to their game, which *I* found offensive, brought my interpretation of the event into question. I had to admit that I was biased when I assumed that Ellen was an unwilling participant in the game.

"I don't know . . . I'm not sure": that response to my question was provocative. Why did I assume she was being manipulated and intimidated? After she responded to my question, I had to consider another scenario: what if these boys, who love gross-out wordplay so much, were trying the game out on Ellen to see what would happen? They knew it would certainly get her attention, but they did not necessarily know how it would affect her. On the other hand, Ellen didn't know how to respond, and so became passive and silent, and (if we remove my immediate perception of helplessness) thoughtful. She was thinking about whether she liked it, because she was a very egalitarian child. She liked girls *and* boys as companions. The boys also liked her as a classmate: she was funny, good natured, intelligent, and verbal. Perhaps they were not working to intimidate her, but simply wanted her attention and resorted to the strategy that had always worked with each other: gross talk.

As I walked away, reflecting on her response, I began to think about how I'd interpreted the event and whether, if I coupled my immediate perception of harassment with Ellen's attitude of thoughtfulness, I might consider the incident as something other than a full-blown act of sexual harrassment. (Yes, I had to admit that I interpreted the act as something tinged with sexuality.) At that point I also began to wonder if I hadn't seen some piece of the origin of what our culture now calls "sexual harrassment." I put that term in quotation marks only to foreground it and call it into question from a researcher's point of view. Perhaps if I watched carefully enough and without bias based on my own life experience, I might see the behavioral roots of a socially and morally charged phrase *in the context of children's play*, where it begins not as a sinister effort to force someone to do something against their will or to subordinate them, but rather as a way to get attention and to explore the boundaries of relationships with the opposite sex.

A few days later in class, Molly came over and told me that the boys were "talking gross again," and said, "We don't like it" ("we" meant Molly, Ellen, Nicki, and Amy, all second-grade girls). I walked over to the table, and of course the boys melted away back to their seats. As I sat down with the girls to ensure that the boys did not return, I asked them why they thought the boys used gross talk.

Molly said, "I think it's because they want to play with us, and they don't know how to get our attention." Then I asked them if it really bothered them a lot.

"Well," responded Ellen, "I think sometimes you like to hear a tiny, little bit of it, but not too much."

"A TINY LITTLE BIT, BUT NOT TOO MUCH"

Of course there's a fine line between "a tiny, little bit" and "not too much." In fact, that is the line that discussions about sexual harrassment focus on. What is provocative about these observations of children is first of all that they open a potential window into the development of sexual misunderstanding between males and females. We know from Tannen's work (1990) that males and females often communicate at cross purposes. We also know that gender differences in children are already very pronounced for most children by age five, although some parents do their darnedest to try and counteract nature and society's influences. Boys and girls are just different. They walk, talk, play, and socialize in different ways. We can mediate some of their tendencies and change how they think about their worlds, but we can't make them the same. Most little boys like gross talk and rough-and-tumble games and hate to sit, while most girls prefer to talk about friends, play domestic games, and sit quietly as they work. When the two sexes begin to want to spend time together, which, from my observation, happens about the middle of the second-grade year (around age 7 or 8), there are many miscommunications. The particular one I've described here is quite typical. There is, however, another side to this coin.

"THE GIRLS ARE BOTHERING US"

In early June of the same year, Tony and Donald came to me at recess to complain that the girls were "bothering" them. I noticed that they were, in fact, being trailed by Amy, Molly, Dierdre, Nicky, and Ellen, who were smiling slyly and keeping a distance of ten feet or so. Tony and Donald recounted how the girls kept following them around, teasing and chasing. This was not a new report; I had been hearing it off and on since spring. However, for some reason I had not acted to curtail it in the same way that I had with Ellen's complaint. That day, however, when we returned to class, I took the whole crew of complaining boys and girls aside and asked them to explain what was happening at recess. Following are audiotaped excerpts from that conversation.

Teacher (to the girls): I've been getting some complaints from boys about girls' behavior on the playground and wanted these boys to describe exactly what's happening so you can hear it and they can tell you what they think of it. Then you can talk back to them about what you think. Okay?

Donald: Well, um, the girls, some of the girls are going, like, "Oh, sorcerers are interesting. Oh, lunatics are interesting," like that, and it's, like, annoying us. And just saying stuff about Ian that makes him mad.

Tom: And it's especially, it's like, especially, like after Ian, kinda like they're doing something bad, and Dierdre's starting to say really *rude* things about us.

Teacher: Can you repeat what she says so that she knows what you're hearing?

Tom: Well, Ian, she said something to Ian. She goes, like, "Doctors are interesting." Like, "My parents are funny. Can *you* cure it?" Like, "The sky is falling, the sky is falling."

Donald: They were bringing over Dierdre, 'cause Deirdre was pretending she was sick and she's, like, yelling, "The sky is falling!" They want Ian to cure her.

I have to admit that I was a bit in the dark about why this would be so upsetting to the boys, but as I listened to the tape later, I realized that for children, references to "doctors" and "curing" someone are risky. As we probably all know from our own childhood, playing doctor is often the first occasion for sexual experimentation. (Now who, I wonder as I write this, is the first to suggest playing doctor?) These boys were certainly getting exercised over the implication of Dierdre's language and behavior, even though I did not find it offensive.

Shortly thereafter, Nicki admitted that some of the histrionics had to do with her.

NICKI: Not that I really really mind it, but, um, when Molly and Ellen are whispering to each other, it kind of annoys me, because now that everyone knows about the love thing, I feel, like, they're talking about me. So it offends me.

IAN: Dierdre is teasing mostly, like, bad stuff about me, like that stuff, like Nicki loves me.

The other girls protested loudly.

NICKI (barely audible): I don't exactly, but I like you.

IAN (refusing to look at Nicki and acknowledge her remark): Yeah, but she's *saying* that she loves me.

The boys continued, complaining that the girls were disrupting their games, and worse, drawing attention to their muscles.

DONALD: Whenever we tried to play a game they come over and start laughing at us and making jokes, and it really bothers us.

TOM: And they stand near us and they're, like, whispering and watching us play, and whispering to each other. It really annoys me.

TONY: And, like, like they say, like, "What was it, that kind of muscle in your arm? What was it? It was some kind of muscle in your arm." And she goes, um, "What was it? Tell us."

Then the conversation shifted and we returned to the girls' side of the story.

MOLLY: I wanna say something. It seems to me that you guys are always having fun with us and teasing us *in* the class, but when we get outside and we're *meant* to be having fun, you seem to, like, not want us around. Why, why are you always playing around in the class and not . . .

DONALD: That's because, that's because outside is when *we* want to be alone.

Molly: Then why won't you let *us* be alone in the classroom?

Nicki: Why do you always have to talk about gross things when we're sitting at the table? You talk about gross things to annoy us and this is our way of getting back.

The boys protested.

Tom: We think it's fun, we're really not trying to . . .

Molly: But what I'm saying is, you're not doing it when you think that we're *not* listening. It's not like we're just a blade of grass. We have feelings.

Dierdre: And you're stepping on us!

Donald: Stepping on you?

Teacher: You mean in the classroom.

Dierdre: Yeah.

Tony: We keep grossing you out because outside you keep annoying us with all of your little . . .

Molly: But you're, the class is *before* we're going out, so you're always starting it up. Why do you keep on doing that? Why do you play around in the classroom and do nothing outside? Why can't you do it the other way around? You get to bother us in here, and then we, and then we get to bother you out there.

Nicki: Yeah, you guys—you discuss your private stuff in the classroom and leave us alone instead of outside. And play around outside instead of in the classroom.

Then Tom tried to explain how the gross-out talk begins.

Tom: When we're grossing you out, we've actually gotten into a conversation, because when we were grossing you out before, we were, like, having fun.

Dierdre: Well, that's the thing with us playing with you. We're having fun, so if we both have fun, then isn't that fair? 'Cause that's what we're doing. You're having fun grossing us out. We're having fun teasing you.

Donald conceded that he, like Ellen, was somewhat ambivalent about the teasing, but he wanted it to stop sometimes: "I've never said I don't like it, but at recess you've heard me say 'Stop, stop teasing!'—like that. You heard me."

The other boys vigorously agreed that Donald had asked the girls to stop before, and so had they. Reluctantly the girls conceded that that was true, they hadn't stopped the teasing, but they insisted that they had asked the boys to stop the gross talk and were only retaliating.

Molly: Yeah, but we're doing that because you do it to us in the class-
room. Especially in the mornings.
Tom: But you don't tell us to stop. You don't tell us.
Ellen: We said "stop" to Donald.
Nicki: Outside, we're just having a bit of fun, and it seems to me that,
that the boys, that boys can already have fun in the mornings.

"WE'RE JUST HAVING A BIT OF FUN"

It seemed to me that these children were presenting the crux of the argument very succinctly. It came down to two factors: differing perceptions
of "fun," and contrasting ideas of when it was appropriate to have fun. As
we have seen, for bad boys, "fun" in the classroom is something they
orchestrate for the purpose of social control. But in this discussion, the
boys were saying that fun for them also had a second aspect of privacy or
intimacy with their own same-sex friends. That kind of fun took place on
the playground at recess.

The girls, however, did not see their personal fun as occurring in the
classroom, and thus they felt that the classroom was clearly an inappro-
priate place for the boys to carry out their idea of fun. In fact, most girls in
the classroom behaved as if they knew that that was not where unstruc-
tured, child-initiated fun takes place. Rather, recess was where the girls
chose to have their fun with the boys. It is interesting to note that their
differing perceptions of where "fun" occurs is where the problems with
managing some boys lies for teachers. Girls seem to understand that the
classroom, while it may be fun and interesting, is not where they initiate
their personal idea of fun, which in this case was chasing, teasing, and
making insinuating remarks about the boys. They initiate that kind of
potentially disruptive play at recess. The boys, though, seem to be defining two kinds of fun in school: one that occurs in the classroom, which is
fun on the level of controlling public discourse and is usually very disruptive; the other, reserved for recess, is for the development of friendships.

So what do we call the girls' actions at recess? Is it teasing, or harassment? If we use Ellen's attitude taken from her earlier remarks and add in
Donald's admission that "I've never said I don't like it," we begin to see a
pattern. These children are not sure what they think about the nature of
the other sex's overtures of friendship. I have concluded, based on my
observation of this particular group, that these children were at all times

playing with their friends. In play, as children always do, they were sorting out their social relationships, and it is almost exactly in the second-grade year that their interest in relating socially to the opposite sex becomes full blown. They know what "fun" is with their same-sex friends; they are trying out that kind of fun on their opposite-sex friends.

RETURNING TO THAT FINE LINE

It is absolutely impossible for me, and has been since I first began observing the development of social relations among these children, to suppress my questions about the ultimate outcomes of their social experiments in adulthood and in society at large. At what point does play become manipulation, or childlike innuendo become menace? In my own life, I have to admit that some men in their attempts to make contact with me (to get my attention?) have made remarks that I consider to be offensive (gross talk?).

I, on the other hand, must confess that in my lifetime I have also intentionally embarrassed (harassed? teased?) a few men, by making pointed references to some part of their body. In doing so I have couched my meaning in metaphors whose intentions were completely readable to the man in question. For example, in one instance I said to a colleague who had just returned from a notoriously male-only golf date, "So, how's your putter?"

Taken literally, that remark is harmless. Taken metaphorically, which includes an interpretation of the tone I used, the remark can be offensive. In this case, the man in question knew exactly what I was referring to, and he was quite embarrassed. The intention of my remark was not flirtatious, and he also knew that. It was a small and unobtrusive retaliation for the ways in which he characteristically treated women in the organization, which I considered to be offensive. But if my remark is more closely examined, it has the same quality as the girls', both in design and in intention: it used an allusion to a private part of his physique to embarrass him. The girls used references to Tony's muscles or to Ian's "cures" to retaliate for the morning gross talk.

Why is it that in nonintimate relationships female innuendo generally continues to be interpreted as teasing, while male innuendo often is interpreted as harassment? I believe the answers to those questions can be found in an examination of the settings in which "fun" originally occurs. For girls, as I've pointed out, most fun of the teasing sort is reserved for recess, and if it spills over into the classroom it is quickly squelched. Most studies of gender in the classroom describe misbehaving by girls as much less tolerated by teachers. From my own experience I would say that is true, not because I am stricter with girls, but rather because they are more responsive to correction.

Boys, however, have their fun in two settings, recess and the classroom, and their fun has two different purposes: manipulation and friendship. In my opinion, men who use harassment as adults are simply continuing a strategy for controlling others that has worked for twelve, sixteen, and possibly even twenty years in an institution (the school) that taught them most everything they know about life. They learn as children that a subtle use of language, both verbal and nonverbal, can bring them power. They learn that other, less dominant boys can also be intimidated by the use of talk that draws attention to their shortcomings.

But girls can be rendered even more passive by the boys' grossing them out. Granted, the gross talk later becomes more sexually explicit language, but that's only because these boys eventually acquire that language and leave the blood-and-guts talk behind. Furthermore, and this makes the interaction with girls much more interesting, some girls, like Ellen, are not sure at first how to interpret the talk, and so they don't always object. Perhaps they think, as Ellen might, that gross talk is an overture of friendship. And if we are being generous, perhaps for some men it is. For other men, however, for the boys of the world who grow up to be powerful men, sophistication and a mastery of *all* the nuances of language are what they have cultivated. They understand, as do the boys, that people can be controlled by very subtle and intelligent uses of language. Some of these men use that language to become leaders; others use it to subordinate, intimidate, and demean. Perhaps as women move into more positions of authority we will find that the same is true of some of them.

AGAIN, THE FINE LINE

Where does the line reside? Thorne (1993) has called this kind of contact across the boundaries of gender "borderwork," and she calls into question whether this is really play.

> Gender boundaries have a shifting presence, but when evoked they are accompanied by stylized forms of action, a sense of performance, mixed and ambiguous meanings (the situations often teeter between play and agression), and heterosexual meanings lurk within other definitions. (p. 66)

Her observations confirm the potential for miscommunication that I have presented here, but they also underscore the necessity for researchers and teachers to examine more closely the work children are doing in their cross-gender play.

I view the children in this book as acting from a healthy motivation to understand their world. I am not able to say more about how each of them eventually uses the knowledge he or she has of social relationships for positive or negative outcomes; those kinds of understandings can come only as more accounts are published about the development of relationships between the sexes in schools. However, I can say from my own personal experience that children need adults to carefully observe and actively participate in their conversations, their manipulations, their performances, and their ruminations about how they want to be treated and how they treat their friends. As a teacher researcher, I am a firm believer in eavesdropping, intervening, questioning, objecting, and problematizing the motives of the children I teach and my own motives. These kinds of interventions, however, require the teacher to uncover the children's understandings while also examining his or her own. We return again to Giroux's desire to "interrogate" the conditions of authority in the classroom, and the exhortation of Grumet: Only when we "study the transferences we bring to the world we know" will we be able to "devise new forms for knowing that will not compel our students to recite the history and future of our desire" (1988, p. 128).

CHAPTER 8

Sing to Your Friends to Make Them Feel Better

Germaine in Sharing Time: October 26

I'm a singer-song.
I'm a singer-song.
Genie, genie, genie, genie,
I'm watching a movie.
Popcorn!

Field Notes: November 11

Germaine has spent the end of this school day writing his phone number on pieces of yellow scrap paper and stuffing it in the children's pockets, inside their books and desks, into their cubbies, and even into my desk drawer. As they leave, he checks to be sure that they've taken his number. What if no one calls?

Observation: December 21

Rachel is making a Christmas card for her grandmother. She goes to a shelf, picks up the box of alphabet stamps and an ink pad, and returns to the table she's sharing with Germaine. As she opens the box and the stamp pad, he looks up, frowns, and says, "What's that? What are those things?" I realize he's never used letter stamps before. Rachel proceeds to give him a detailed demonstration and gets him a piece of paper to make his own card.

Germaine's Writing: March 14

My scol is a speshoe scol. I like it becaues we do wrck.
my clas is smart they teach me sometime The end.

[My school is a special school. I like it because we do work.
My class is smart. They teach me sometime. The end.]

When Germaine joined my class in its second year, he was one of eleven other new students who had not been with me as first graders. Eleven children from the prior year were continuing with me as second graders, and together with these eleven newcomers we formed a new class. From the time I met him, Germaine, who was African American, seemed extremely reserved and almost aloof from the other children, even those he knew from the previous year. As I observed and interacted with him, however, I could see that he was very interested in becoming friends with his classmates, but was unsure of how to proceed. Finally he made some attempts to connect, always using a technique like the phone numbers he'd observed the other children employing with success. I never saw him ask someone directly to play with him or to sit with him at lunch or in a meeting.

Unlike many of his peers, Germaine's persona in the classroom was always the same. It did not change depending on the context of his interactions, like that of so many other children, but was rather more intense and focused. He was maintaining a single approach, or playing a continuous role: he presented himself to the world as a dignified, restrained, and serious individual. However, although he did not engage in the performances of the class as a whole, his choice to stand apart could also be seen as a performance, albeit a solo one. He stayed in character regardless of the dynamics of his interactions with other children.

I believe this role concealed Germaine's perception that he did not know how to navigate the social terrain of this classroom; sometimes he was not even familiar with the objects (such as the stamp pad and letters) his classmates took for granted. His heritage, culture, and language style were all very different from those of most of his classmates. Germaine's decision to stay outside the stream of social dramas might have come from his correct perception of that difference. Although, as I have pointed out, the class was racially mixed, there was only one other African-American child, Latia. Germaine's and Latia's positions in class were similar: their lives outside school were in direct contrast to those of most of the other children.

Germaine was from a working class family with ten children living in the house. Both parents worked long hours, and Germaine was cared for after school by a variety of older siblings, aunts, and uncles. Germaine did not have a lot of toys and books; his family did not own a computer; he did not routinely watch videos. He had not attended kindergarten at our school and had not gone to preschool. His weekends were filled with visits to and from his large extended family, pick-up basketball and football games, and the communal making of meals. If he interacted with his class-mates outside of school, it was during a soccer practice, or the result of a chance meeting in the park.

Most of my other students were Caucasians from middle- and upper-middle-class homes with professional parents, and most went to daycare after school. Each had one or two siblings and was economically comfort-able. Most had gone to preschool for 2 or 3 years and had attended our kindergarten, and all had many books, tapes, videos, a computer, and computer games. Their weekends were filled with trips to museums or artistic events, excursions to outdoor nature preserves, and play dates with classmates. Their parents spent a good amount of time planning and orchestrating opportunities for the children to spend time together out-side of school.

Although it is easy for adults to say that children are children, and thus, being childlike, will naturally have a great deal in common where play and imagination occur, this assumption is simplistic. Children of different races, cultures, and classes do not necessarily share a common imaginative lan-guage that enables them to play and perform together. Play and perfor-mance are based on shared understandings of the subject matter and the social and psychological issues being played out. Children do not easily explore social dynamics together if their experiences of society, language, culture, and the family are tremendously different. There was, in fact, a social topography in our classroom that Germaine was not familiar with. He was quite perceptive about what he didn't know and chose a cautious approach to navigating the social terrain.

BEING DIFFERENT

When considering friendships and how they are formed and ruptured, it is clear that the issue of difference is a big one. For schoolchildren, differ-ence can reside in the color of your skin, the language you speak, the ac-cent you speak it with, how you dress, whether you have a learning prob-lem or a physical handicap, or even the food you bring for lunch. That is not to say that children are naturally alienated by differences. Rather they find them curious, something to study, a condition to be scrutinized. In my experience it is only when another more powerful individual directs their attention to the difference as something to be ashamed of that chil-dren take up that opinion.

During most of the school year Germaine maintained his very digni-fied but distant persona. It was clear that although he was well liked by the other children, there were many issues that separated him from them in significant ways. Germaine enjoyed being in class but viewed his family members as his friends, and on the playground he would choose to play with his cousins or stepbrother rather than a classmate. Further, although he was respected by the other children for his skill as an athlete, Germaine was a delayed reader and did not excel academically. His skills as a soccer and baseball player were his main source of achievement as a 7-year-old, and as soon as he entered school the other children, primarily boys, made note of it and gave him credit for it. Nonetheless, even at 6 or 7 years of age, those children also knew that physical talent didn't have the same value *in the classroom* as being an early reader or excelling at math. They had already internalized the prevailing cultural ethic that while physical intelligence and giftedness might gain you notoriety and lots of money, it did not gain overall respect. Those talents were compartmentalized into the "sports thing." Germaine may have been a great athlete, but that didn't mean he was a really "valuable" companion in class. In fact, his delays as a reader made him a less valuable companion, so he was somewhat marginalized in many academic activities.

STUDYING CLASSROOM TOPOGRAPHY

When I observed Germaine with the other children in class, I saw that he was watching every detail of their interactions very closely. He seemed to be studying even the social protocols of the classroom and would not participate in an activity carried out by a child or an adult until he understood his role completely. There were occasions when the words other children used were unfamiliar to him. In essence, even the assumption that he as an English speaker shared a common language with my other English speakers was called into question. I saw, as I had with other African-American children I had taught, that Germaine spoke black English, a different dialect than that spoken by my middle-class Caucasian children. There were times, therefore, when his social maneuverings became more difficult, not because the other children didn't respect his words, but rather because they did not always share his deeper contextual meanings. For example, one day during sharing time, Eli was showing a wooden chessboard and the pieces that went with it. When he called on Germaine for a question, Germaine said, "Is that thing the same as the other thing?" A silence fell as we tried to figure out what Germaine was referring to. I asked him to repeat his question, and as he rephrased it, "Is that thing the same as the other thing we have over there?", he pointed to our games area. Then Eli realized he was referring to the plastic chess game across the room, and answered in the affirmative.

After I related this conversation to my 19-year-old son, Liam, the evening after it happened, he pointed out that Germaine's phrasing was very similar to that used when an individual is speaking a foreign language and trying to name an object not encountered before. The use of the word "thing" is quite a common substitution for new language speakers because they don't have all the vocabulary necessary to name objects in their environments. I have often heard African-American children refer to an object they have just encountered for the first time in school as "that thing." Frequently, well-meaning teachers become worried by this inexact usage and refer such children for speech and language services. It represents to me a clear instance of the kinds of difficulties that cultural differences, which manifest themselves in languge gaps, present to children like Germaine in school. Germaine knew the name of the plastic chess set we used in the class; the more ornate wooden set did not, to him, naturally go by the same name.

When we teachers described Germaine, we always remarked on what a good, sweet little boy he was. That impression didn't come from our sense that he was submissive and would do whatever we told him (actually, he wouldn't do something if he didn't understand its purpose and value), but rather from the fact that he was a person of high moral purpose. He was unusually altruistic; he was never greedy or vindictive, was always polite, and seemed unusually respectful of others. His demeanor, however, was a source of contrast and contradiction when compared with the behavior of many of his classmates. Coming from a background where he had so much less than they in material goods, he displayed an attitude of restraint and generosity in situations where his peers would often be gluttonous and greedy.

When, for example, the children wrote out their New Year's resolutions, Germaine, unlike most of his classmates, had no difficulty understanding that resolutions were not things other people should do for you, but rather things you'd resolve to undertake to improve yourself as a person or do for others. When the assignment was given, Germaine quickly wrote not one but five resolutions:

1. Walk away from fights.
2. Buy more presents for my mom and dad.
3. Shake hands with my friends.
4. Don't shake hands with people you don't know.
5. Sing to your friends to make them feel better.

It was not surprising, therefore, that after the children got to know Germaine, they just plain liked him. He was a good companion and a reliable friend. But although they tried to include him in their stories and their elaborate social ruses, he rarely joined them. The machinations of boy-and-girl playground conflicts, or the verbal one-upsmanship of the children, seemed foreign territory to Germaine; he always maintained a safe distance from any ambiguous social situations where he could not be sure of the outcome. As a result he was not a co-actor with the other children and usually maintained the position of an observer in classroom events, unless the event was so hilarious and foolish that he couldn't restrain himself. And then he would allow himself only the smallest visible foray into laughter and joy.

GERMAINE AND SHARING

Field Notes: November 16

> For sharing, Germaine brings in a model of a jumbo jet his mother just gave him. As he begins, Peggy [the office assistant] comes in from the office and tells me he's not supposed to be in school today because he's sick. His mother, who thought he was home in bed, discovered that he got up, got dressed, and walked to school, apparently to be sure he didn't miss his sharing day. Peggy waits until he finishes taking questions and comments from the class, then we pack him up and send him home to bed.

There was only one classroom routine that Germaine participated in from early on in the year, and that was sharing time. He realized quite early that these sessions were an opportunity. Without fail, on his designated sharing day Germaine would get up into the chair and tell a story. Sometimes he told a true story, but more often than not, he made one up on the spot. By October, I had begun to keep careful track of his stories because they were so different from those told by his classmates, reflecting his particular background and language history. He quickly gained a foothold with his classmates because of their fascination and delight with that difference. My field notes record Germaine's first experience with sharing time:

Field Notes: October 5

> Germaine decides to get in the chair. He climbs up (it is quite tall for him) and sits there silently (afraid?). His legs dangle, and he stares quite deeply into my eyes for about 30 seconds. I say, "Take

your time." Andrew adds in, "We've got all the time in the world." Then Josie, "Yeah." And Eli, "Right." Germaine begins. (The line breaks indicate Germaine's phrasing and pace.)

One time it was a big pumpkin.
It was in the grass.
It keep on saying,
"I'm hurt, I'm hurt."
The witch came,
and then it was a porcupine.
It came up
and gave the witch those things.

Another child adds: "Prickles, poking things." Germaine nods.

The witch told the pumpkin to go get her broom,
and gave the porcupine warts.
Then it was Andrew
who went to go get the witch.

Germaine continued along these lines for several minutes, gradually expanding the story until it included "the whole school," naming many children in the class as characters. As he continued his voice became louder, his diction and inflection were sharp and varied, and he portrayed different characters by changing the pitch and tone of his voice. By the end, all of the children were pointing to themselves when he looked at them, signaling that they wanted to be in the story.

It became clear as the weeks passed that although Germaine's stories seemed disjointed in their development, jumping from one scenario to another, they were always compelling because he included his classmates as central characters. These were not linear stories, beginning with a problem and then proceeding logically toward the problem's resolution, but were rather what I would call circular stories, creating intertextual relationships among many aspects of his own and the other children's lives, and representing many characteristics of African-American storytelling (Abrahams, 1976; Bauman, 1977; Dyson, 1993; Heath, 1983; Smitherman, 1986). His progression, for example, might take pieces of *The Wizard of Oz* (a version of which he had been reading earlier in the week), part of a fake story about sharks Nathaniel had told the day before, and the approach of an upcoming holiday, and spin them all together into a new scenario and time frame. Germaine's stories just grabbed inspiration from everywhere, but most especially from his classmates.

These early traits in his storytelling style were refined as the weeks passed. I soon saw that Germaine was the only child in my class who told inclusive stories. He deliberately included as many of his classmates as possible (and sometimes even their family members, if he had met them), as well as class pets like Violet, our bunny, and my intern and myself. Several subplots in the story ran at the same time, and just when I thought Germaine had forgotten an earlier strand of action, he would draw it back in with a new device like a joke or a song.

For example, in early December, Germaine's story had three clear subplots:

1. Daniel had been naughty and couldn't get any toys from Santa.
2. Allen pulled out all his teeth, and couldn't figure out how to get them back in.
3. Santa was a fake and everyone in the class kept becoming him.

Late in the story, he very casually paused, looked around at his audience, and said: "Then . . . Daniel swallowed Allen's eyebrow!"

That reminded us of the early plot and broke up the audience as the image of Allen, already without his teeth, was now in danger of losing his eyebrows as well. A few lines later, Germaine sang a ditty from out of the blue to introduce me as another Santa pretender.

"Then Karen and Eli came skipping, skippety doo, skippety dee."

Germaine seemed to pluck these little rockets of silliness, sound, and song from the air, but somehow they always pulled the story together. His style reminded me of Merleau-Ponty's sense that "words, vowels, and phonemes are so many ways of 'singing' the world, and . . . their function is to represent things . . . because they extract and literally express their emotional essence" (1964, p.187). Germaine's stories were like long, circular, and inclusive "talk-songs"(Smitherman, 1986, p. 137) that expressed his alert and affectionate personality and the richness of his oral tradition.

There was no question in my mind that this was the one recurring point in his week when Germaine broke out of his steady, unchanging persona and orchestrated a performance with many parts. His performance, however, while it elicited participation from his audience, was still a solo in that he told the story, became the characters, and controlled the action. His imaginal world included everyone, but he did not allow others to take control of that world. The effects on the class were, to borrow a term from Beatrix Potter, "soporific" (1909). All of us ended up feeling so tickled and pleased by the fluency of his associations that we'd chuckle and chuckle and chuckle, and soon be giggling, then dreamy; and finally we'd realize that Germaine had been telling us a story for twenty minutes and we needed to stop and go on to the next person. Essentially, our awareness of time and place vanished. Germaine's use of sound, song, and tone lured everyone into the story; even children who understood little English would be smiling and dreamy, rubbing their eyes as if they'd been asleep. (As Smitherman points out, "Songified patterns [in African-American discourse] reach down to the 'deep structure' of life, that common level of shared human expression" 1986, p. 135.)

But equally as compelling was our understanding that Germaine never forgot who was sitting in front of him. For him, storytelling was inherently a social action that reached out to embrace his classmates and was completely dependent on the responsiveness of his audience. His linguistic and metaphoric playfulness, and the responsibility he took for including everyone in every story, were enthralling. He caught our attention because he paid such careful attention to our life in the classroom, our reactions to his intentions as a storyteller, and our response to his words. As Germaine came to know more members of the class, elements of their lives entered his stories. He included Josie's mother, who drove him to soccer, Latia's older brother and his exploits, Mia's broken glasses, and Marcus's X-Men cards. He acknowledged a new Japanese student's confusion about his arrival in this country, included another child's friend from a different class, and mentioned the universal drama of losing a tooth. Any important person or event in a classmate's life would eventually end up in one of his stories.

Outside the sharing time format, however, he always went back to his role as the reserved, watchful, and respectful classmate. His forays into drama were carefully contained in the once-a-week event of sharing time. However, as the year progressed, there was a level of comfort with his teachers and a few classmates that gradually grew for him in private encounters. It became clear that he was funny even outside the sharing chair, but that, unlike his fantastic sharing time stories, his understanding of the world was grounded in real life stories from which he took clear moral lessons.

Germaine (to me one morning): We got a friend. His name is Green Boy.
Teacher: Green Boy! What a funny name. Why do you call him Green Boy?
Germaine (laughing with me): I don't know. We just do . . . he's not green, I know that. But he's sort of bad. He's got in trouble before 'cause he hurt someone.

Such brief exchanges always contained a kernel of information and reflection, but those clearer pictures of the real Germaine were kept concealed from most of the other children. This reserve in some ways protected him because he could not be drawn into social exchanges he might not control, but it also made him vulnerable in ways we were soon to discover.

GERMAINE AND THE BAD BOYS

Artful performances in particular illustrated the vulnerability of the performer, who puts forward not simply a text, but the self. A positive or negative reaction from the audience is a response to that self, a granting or withholding of respect.

—Dyson (1993, p. 73)

Normally, the other children respected Germaine's position as an outsider. The only children who occasionally tried to pull him into a risky interaction were, as one might expect, the bad boys. On occasion Germaine became the object of those boys' attention, an event which we have seen is not usually a positive one. We saw in Chapter 3 how Germaine was slighted by Andrew, but there were other events I witnessed that clarified both the extremity of bad boy behavior and the hazards children like Germaine might encounter even though they worked very hard to stay out of the nebulous and sometimes risky events of classroom life. In fact, if I honestly consider why Germaine, of all children, was subjected to the bad boys' aggression, I have to conclude it was not because he was African American and they were racist, but rather because his talent at entertaining the class and orchestrating sharing time gave him a clout and power within class that was, because of his personal distance and reserve, difficult to break through or challenge.

One day in early May, Michael came to school with some of his home collection of X-Men cards. (These depict fantasy superheroes and were collected by boys who had enough spending money.) Germaine was very interested in the cards and asked Michael if he could look at them with him. They spent the time before school started meticulously examining the cards and discussing their merits. When I called the children to meeting, Michael generously gave Germaine five of the cards to keep. Germaine took the cards and put them carefully in his back pocket, checking several times to be sure they were still there.

At sharing time that morning, Mia went first. She showed a new book, and then, after a few questions, said she was "waiting for a question." This was a well-known signal to the group that she was waiting for a particular question, usually an inquiry about a child's favorite thing. One of the girls asked, "Will you show us your favorite page?" and Mia did. Then she asked the children if they wanted her to read the page. They did, and she read the page with great energy and expression. (She was a very talented reader.)

Germaine's turn to share followed. He carefully pulled the cards out of his pocket and climbed into the chair. He was obviously very proud of the cards and described with great dignity and just a hint of a smile of pride how Michael had given them to him. Michael grinned broadly and seemed quite pleased with himself. At that point he moved closer to Germaine, sitting directly to his left. As he did that I noticed that Andrew glanced over at Michael, stared for a minute, and then moved from the back to the center of the group, sitting directly in front of Germaine. [I noted this seemingly insignificant detail in my field notes because I had adopted the belief that when children deliberately reposition themselves in a group that has already settled, the physical act signals an intention of some sort. I had, as the reader might imagine, become particularly attentive to the movements of the bad boys because I knew that very little of what they did was without a purpose.]

Germaine went on to tell about each card, and, with Michael's help, read the names of each character. Then, according to the sharing protocol, he asked for questions and comments from his audience. After a few questions, Germaine said, as Mia had, "I'm waiting for a question." At that point Andrew's hand shot up, and Germaine called on him.

Andrew said, "I think this is the one you've been waiting for. Can you *read* your favorite card?" Without missing a beat, Germaine turned over a card and began to try and read it. I realized immediately that Germaine had been set up, but from Germaine's immediate response I was not sure he knew that he'd been entrapped. He held the cards close to his face as he tried to read the tiny print, painstakingly sounding out the bizarre names and advanced vocabulary. As he labored, Michael, who had memorized the text of all his X-Men cards, sometimes called out the next difficult word, or got up on his knees, peered over Germaine's shoulder, and quietly prompted him. Meanwhile, the rest of the audience, including me, watched in almost stunned silence.

Some children glanced nervously at me as Germaine labored. I was watching him intensely, trying to figure out how he'd gotten so trusting that he'd try such an impossible thing, debating what I could do about it without humiliating him. Five minutes passed and still Germaine continued painstakingly to sound out each word on the card. The words, parsed into sounds, soon lost their meaning, but still the group was silent. There was no movement, no coughing or whispering. I wondered what the children were thinking. Andrew was sitting very still, staring straight at Germaine. Finally, I said quietly to Germaine that we had run out of time, hoping he would take that opportunity to be rescued, but instead he looked up and said, "but I only have one more [sentence] left." I nodded that he should go on, and he finished the sentence.

To ease the tension, I asked him if he would show the back of the card so that the other children could see the size of the print. He turned the card over and displayed it, moving it slowly from one side of the group to the other, stopping pointedly in the middle of the group where Andrew sat. Just then, Andrew said under his breath, but audibly enough for me to hear from where I sat at the back of the group, "I wouldn't have had any trouble reading that." None of the children looked at him or acknowledged his comment. I made a monumental effort to restrain myself from answering him back.

Before I could call an end to the session, Germaine asked for more questions and comments. He called on Nathaniel, who said, quite deliberately, "Can you *show* us your favorite card?"

"*That*," said Germaine, "is the question I was waiting for," and he pulled out the card, turned it over, and displayed the picture.

This was, perhaps, one of the most malicious stunts I had seen in a long time. It embodied the way in which bad boys sometimes use their knowledge of a classroom ritual to manipulate a naive and unsuspecting child. Andrew, who was a superior reader and had his own X-Men cards, knew exactly how difficult the text on the cards was to read: how small the print was, and how complicated and unusual the language. He had just seen Germaine struggle to read the name at the top of each card. In this case, Andrew took the question he knew Germaine was waiting for, and then, by manipulating the wording and juxtaposing it to Mia's response to the question, used it to humiliate Germaine. He took Germaine's pride and happiness in Michael's gesture of friendship and turned it into a moment of anxiety and stress.

Of course, one might say that I was simply projecting my interpretation of the situation onto Germaine. But I believe, based on Germaine's response to Nathaniel ("*That* is the question I was waiting for") and the way he so deliberately showed Andrew the size of the print, that he understood what Andrew had done, but chose, as always, to try and maintain his sense of dignity and respectfulness. For several months, Andrew had observed, as we all had, that when Germaine chose to sit in the chair and share, he did so with pride. Germaine was always visibly conscious of the privilege of sitting in front of his classmates and directing the flow of the conversation. He never took his time in the teacher's chair for granted or used it frivolously. Andrew's ability to perceive those details would have led him to conclude that Germaine, unlike another, less dignified child, would never answer his question by saying he couldn't read the card, but would rather, from a point of dignity, try to honor Andrew's request.

ALTERING THE BALANCE OF POWER

There is another strand in this incident that is unusual and should be considered for what it says about other children and their social intentions. Michael, a very bad boy most of the time, considered Germaine to be a friend, and only he, of all of us, found a way to support Germaine in that difficult situation. As Germaine struggled, Michael immediately assisted him with a matter-of-fact air that signaled he placed no value on the fact that Germaine could not read the cards. But further complicating the scenario is my perception that Michael's behavior, early in the sharing session, had obviously contributed to Andrew's decision to ask the question. Could it be that Andrew resented Michael's morning alliance with Germaine?

Sometimes when I imagine what goes on in the bad boys' heads, I envision that they have a giant hierarchical diagram of the children in the class (and the teachers), and each day they reconfigure it, depending on who they perceive to be standing at the top, or, to put it in my framework, who orchestrates the best performance. This time Michael had somewhat altered the diagram by devoting the early morning to a confidential X-Men conversation with Germaine. Michael, who loved those cards, placed great value on the interests of others in his collection. Andrew, as a more typical bad boy, would never get too excited about anything owned by anyone, including himself. That was not a cool way to be in school.

But Michael was atypical in this one aspect. When he was interested in something, he was passionate about it and attempted to use his influence to pull everyone else along with him. (Of course, the "something" was usually of his own choosing. For him, it was not cool to be excited about anything a teacher might propose.) If a child or an adult responded, he would look upon them with very benevolent eyes, and he would consider them to be a friend—thus his generosity to Germaine.

But the diagram had been altered both by this alliance and by Germaine's prior success as a storyteller. When Germaine called the class's attention to Michael's gesture by sharing his new cards, his action, however innocently conceived, could not pass unnoticed. In this case, Germaine did not understand, I think, what he was doing to the social balance of the classroom. His lack of engagement with the day-to-day social dynamics of the class left him unprepared for the consequences of making what might be perceived by others to be a direct entry into the clique of bad boys.

I cannot emphasize too strongly here how carefully bad boys scrutinize each and every exchange. Their ability to analyze the meanings behind words and gestures is very highly developed. As I've pointed out, they have a superior understanding of the social context of language, a skill that only gets honed over the years in school. But their scrutiny goes beyond just taking note of the meanings of exchanges, because every child does that. The bad boy's scrutiny includes a constant evaluation of whether someone else's action depletes some of his own personal social currency. As I noted in my description of this event, "Andrew glanced over at Michael, *stared for a minute,* and then moved from the back to the center of the group." This observation is quoted directly from my field notes, and my noting of the stare is significant. That stare embodied the evaluative *subtextual* act. Most probably Andrew did not know at that point what he was going to do, but the stare represented the realization that he needed to do something to rectify the hierarchy. In some ways his question to Germaine was intended to devalue both Germaine's worth as a person, and Michael's gesture of friendship: how could Michael have given his treasured cards to someone who couldn't even read them?

And what of the other children observing this dilemma? As I've noted before, sometimes bad boys lose control over their scenarios. This is one case where, rather than gaining ground from his actions, Andrew lost it. As the event progressed, it was clear that he had violated the rule of supporting the sharer in a most shocking way. None of the children enjoyed Germaine's struggle or shared Andrew's contempt. In fact, their affect during the incident, and Nathaniel's very carefully worded question "Can you *show* us your favorite card?", signaled that Andrew had gone too far. From that time on, though, sharing time was more difficult for Germaine. Although every other child in the room supported him when he got in the chair and paid close attention, the bad boys had decided that he was a target, and he rarely escaped their scrutiny.

CHARTING A SAFE COURSE

"my clas is smart they tech me sometime"

—*Germaine*

Our classroom was unfamiliar and a bit perilous for Germaine. But he needed to learn about the dynamics of our social relations no matter how complex and uncomfortable the process might be. Classmates were teaching him lessons at many levels; even his time in the sharing chair, depending on the kind of exchange he initiated, had the potential to instruct him in the vagaries of being a "boy" in the culture of the classroom. It did not matter if Germaine was a white boy or a black boy here. It mattered only that the dramas some boys set in motion were qualitatively different from the dramas of other boys or girls, and he needed to understand the nature of all of those dramas to move comfortably in the world of school. There was no way for Germaine to script all his interactions with his classmates so that he could control their outcomes. The desire to belong required forays into the unknown, even if he lost his way.

GERMAINE: Karen, have you ever been lost?

KAREN: Sure, I've been lost before.

GERMAINE: And were you scared?

KAREN: When I was lost? Yeah, sometimes when I get lost, I am scared.

GERMAINE: Have your husband ever said he was going to come and pick you up, and he didn't come?

KAREN: Yes, once that happened.

GERMAINE: And did you think he forgot?

KAREN: Well, I didn't know. I was worried that something happened to him.

GERMAINE: Like he got stabbed or something?

KAREN: Yeah, like he was hurt.

GERMAINE: Did you think he was stabbed or maybe shot with a gun?

KAREN: Sometimes I do worry about that, or maybe that he's had an accident.

GERMAINE: Once my Dad got in a accident. He got knocked off his bike. But he was O.K. now.

CHAPTER 9

"What Does That Mean, the 'N' Word?"

It is not overlap that creates interruptions but conversational moves that wrench a topic away from another speaker's course.

—Tannen (1990, p. 214)

Field Notes: May 22

For some reason the bad boys are jerking Germaine around again. As he sits down in the chair to share, Andrew moves right up to the chair, sort of hunching in front of Germaine so he can't really move his legs. Then I hear Andrew say under his breath, "You know, we're not going to wait." He is referring to the long time Germaine takes before he begins his stories. I hear the remark and call Andrew on it, saying I am surprised to hear him say that when he knows we would all wait for him. Andrew looks away but doesn't move. I ask him to move back so that Germaine has some space. He does so. Germaine begins the story. It's a very carefully conceived story about how some of the boys went to a basketball game. Germaine names the teams, the star players from the NBA, where the game is taking place, etc. I am impressed that Germaine is so focused and clear in setting up the plot. I look around and notice Charles. He is sitting staring at Germaine with his chin propped up on his hands. His face is a mask: he looks at Germaine unblinking, unsmiling, *completely* unresponsive to anything Germaine says, even as other children laugh or respond. (Germaine has not included Charles in his story this week . . . any connection?) Michael is to Germaine's direct left. He is playing with a piece of fluff, blowing it around, commenting as he often will in a low voice on words Germaine uses, or his choice of players. It's always a corrective comment, or a suggestion for a change in the plot. I feel like Germaine is under a lot of pressure. He's got three powerful boys at his feet, fixing him with intimidating, unresponsive stares and wisecracks that only he can hear.

What Germaine does is to subtly change his story so that these boys, especially Michael and Andrew, become the center of the story. Then he puts Charles in. This bothers me because I see he's picking up what I am sensing, and changing his style to mollify or cater to these boys. It ticks me off that they can manipulate him like this. I'm also ticked off because what they do is so quiet that I can't in any way intervene without taking away from Germaine's time in the chair. I can't put my finger on what I'm seeing because it's so nebulous, and I want to believe these boys are too young to know consciously what they are doing. I wonder why they are doing it, and why I've put these notes in my *Gender* notebook. I guess it's because this is a bad *boy* behavior. They do it to anyone who in some way has a different and persuasive voice: teachers, Germaine, certain girls.

As I reviewed these notes, pondering the manipulations that my bad boys had used, I wondered again about their motives. Perhaps I could say that the only consistent factor I saw influencing, for example, Andrew's or Charles's behaviors was that evaluative or banking approach to power, their desire to control the discourse. If anyone threatened their authority, that person was then a probable target. As we have seen from the last chapter, Germaine's style of maintaining his separateness, his misunderstanding of social protocols, and his reputation as a very entertaining and inclusive storyteller made him very vulnerable. Similarly, Dierdre's power and popularity as a beautiful girl made her constantly vulnerable, as we saw in Chapter 5. Daniel's excellence as an athlete made him temporarily vulnerable. Each of these children was compromised precisely because of the threat he or she posed to the bad boys' authority.

So perhaps there is not clear evidence for racism or sexism with children this age. Maybe what I was observing was simply a desire for social power. However, regardless of what I call it, it is important to consider how this kind of power play affects children like Germaine. He has dark skin and lives in a different cultural milieu than almost every other child in the class, and the fact remains that Germaine's situation of being marginalized is experienced by many other African-American children in this country who find themselves as the minority in a racially mixed classroom. In a similar sense, the same situation is experienced by every non-Caucasian immigrant child now in our schools.

Even when a class of children is racially mixed, as mine is, the predominant culture and reality present and promoted in the classroom is that of the white middle class. In fact, even in classes where the majority of children are African American, Hispanic, or immigrants from other third world countries, the predominant culture and reality represented and promoted in the classroom is still that of the *white middle class*. That is both because most teachers are from the white middle class, and because many schools clearly promote white middle-class culture. I have observed that working-class Caucasian children also struggle to figure out where they are and what the rules of behavior are. But their skin is not brown, and while they also hold themselves apart from the classroom dramas, they do so only as long as is necessary to understand the different nuances of the social dynamics. Then they are able to join in because they share a common language and many aspects of mainstream American culture. Home culture, for a child like Germaine, is a vast construct encompassing language, values, social protocols, family dynamics, and many aspects of daily life, and it is not the same as the home culture of most of his friends.

For Germaine, therefore, how he was in school was influenced not only by his gender, but also by his skin color. Gender and race were inseparable from each other in this context. (This point has been emphasized by other writers. See, for example, Best, 1983; Thorne, 1993; Williams, 1991.) The few times when Germaine took a risk and tried to enter the culture of his white peers, he took the chance of getting hurt. His experience was that he had to be vigilant and careful of how he presented himself in class. When he realized that he was effective as a storyteller and used his time in sharing to develop that skill, he began to encounter the kinds of resistance to his performance that I have just described. Thus, precisely because he was uninitiated in certain mainstream cultural protocols, he learned that, unlike the other children, if *he* were to initiate a performance, it could have a different outcome than he'd intended. His intention, like that of many of the children, was to entertain and to make a social bond with his audience; that, however, was not the intention of the bad boys. As a result, he began to alter his own personal position as a storyteller to suit the needs of his powerful classmates. Finally, a few weeks after the incident recorded above, Germaine stopped using his sharing time for storytelling, although he did not stop sharing. In effect he pulled back, taking something that he did well but that made him vulnerable, and suppressed it rather than using the opportunity to develop it. Children alter their behavior or assume public selves as a result of very subtle encounters in their world. In some cases, their behavior changes to tolerate more risks as a social being; in others, it changes to minimize risk. So we might say that although we cannot attribute the bad boys' behaviors to racism we can say that the dynamics they set in motion illuminate the precariousness of Germaine's, or any other African-American child's, life in school. Eventually those dynamics may come to be associated with racial differences and exclusion.

ELI

As another example of these dynamics, let me describe two incidents that one of Germaine's classmates set in motion at the end of his second year with me. Eli, who was Caucasian, had been in my class for two years. He entered as a very young first grader who had many babyish behaviors, but he was quite articulate. During his first-grade year, Eli was very happy in class. He formed close friendships with Andrew and Josie and deeply emulated Tony and Tom. When he entered second grade, however, something had changed in his relationship with his friends. As Andrew, Michael, and Charles became more dominant in class, Eli had difficulty maintaining his close relationship with Andrew. Josie, who had only boy friends, continued to be a close friend to Eli, but Andrew was no longer willing to include Eli in their games. As an additional contrast, Eli was a late reader, and his delay became more obvious as the other children made steady progress in their reading. Andrew and Josie, in fact, were excellent readers and shared a deep interest in books, often reading the same ones at school and at home. Eli could participate in their discussions only if he had the same book read to him by his parents (which was arranged for a while), and the issue of his reading soon became an additional factor in the friendship.

Some people like to say that boys can play with lots of friends at one time, while girls will fight if more than two of them play a game. Their descriptions of girls in threesomes conjure up images of two girls whispering secrets about the other while she sulks. Oddly enough, this was exactly the kind of scenario that Eli found himself in. It was not Josie, however, who ultimately orchestrated the tension in the triad. Neither Eli nor Andrew seemed able to share her. They both coveted their time with Josie, while she, the girl, was quite eager to play with both of them. Thus she found herself in the middle of an intense struggle to monopolize her attention. She confessed to me several times that she liked them both and wished they could just all play "like normal kids."

Josie did not seem to care that Eli was young or that he couldn't read. Andrew, however, used those traits to harass Eli. If the class was having a silent reading period, Andrew sometimes picked up his chapter book, took a seat near Eli (who was usually sitting with Josie), and leaned over Eli's shoulder to see what he was reading. Early in the year, Eli selected simple reading books that were appropriate for his reading level, but when Andrew saw the kind of book he was reading, he drew attention to it and made goofy faces at Josie and any other friends who sat close by. I, like the other children in the area, overheard Andrew's questions and asides to Eli: "Why are you reading such a simple book?" or "I read that in kindergarten." Silent reading, although quiet, is a public time for reading that differs from reading instruction in small groups. Every child in class can see what every other child chooses for reading material in silent reading, and children are urged by their teachers to choose books that are at a comfortable reading level.

At first, in an effort to be casual, Eli shrugged and put the book away, then went back and pretended to read over Andrew's or Josie's shoulder. After a few weeks, however, I noticed that Eli was "reading" chapter books during silent reading, books he could not possibly have read on his own, but that looked impressive. When Andrew saw Eli's new strategy, he changed his approach. He sidled over to Eli, settled himself down next to him on the rug, and casually put his own book aside. "Eli," he'd say, "I love that book, let's read it together. You read one page, and I'll read the next." Eli would smile and demur, then move away to a new seat, leaving Josie and Andrew to read alone. He was a very proud child.

Best (1983), in her study of gender relations in an elementary school where she was a reading specialist, has described the relationship between poor reading achievement and exclusion from peer groups among boys. "The boys who were rejected from peer group membership lost macho points because they were reading 'baby' books—first- and second-grade readers" (p. 22). Boys who were delayed readers and were excluded from peer groups, simultaneously lost their desire to improve, and made few gains. "The concerns of the rejected boys themselves was far less with their academic progress or lack of it than with their inability to achieve acceptance in their peer world" (p. 51). Best describes how, for this kind of boy, the lack of acceptance often led to antisocial behavior and real depression, and notes that this dynamic operated *only* for boys. She also reports observing "fake liking" only among boys, a phenomenon in which they would pretend to like someone for social purposes.

It soon became apparent that Eli was losing his place in the friendship. And with that loss of place came a loss of status in the class, because Eli would not give up ground to Andrew, as most other children would. He made the struggle a public struggle, and he usually came out the loser. For the entire year Eli wanted to be recognized as a part of the group of powerful boys and deliberately orchestrated encounters for that purpose. At times the boys included Eli in their plans, but then they repudiated him the next day. More often than not the repudiation took place, as we would expect, in a public context. It was not the private silencing that girls might deliver to a no longer useful friend, but rather always occurred in front of other children in class.

Andrew, as we know, was a very powerful bad boy. He was not willing to be friends with someone based on a history of a friendship in kindergarten and first grade. His new role as a dominant child required more selective friendships, primarily with other bad boys like Charles and Michael—and, of course, with Josie. Each day the tension between Eli and Andrew grew worse. As class lined up to go to lunch, a struggle over who lined up next to Josie often ensued between Andrew and Eli, sometimes ending in shoving and pushing, and always involving Andrew's other friends as antagonists. At recess, if Eli succeeded in sitting with Josie and the boys, they orchestrated a game Eli was not invited to play. Eli followed the group around, trying to make an entry into the game by using clever verbal arguments, but he was always rebuffed. Each time he was told he couldn't play, he engaged the boys in an elaborate analysis of why he, as opposed to other children, couldn't play, and thereby stalled their game. Josie could be seen in the crowd, wanting to get on with the game, but separate from the repartee.

On other days Eli made plans with Josie before school to play with him and a few other friends at lunch, and Andrew returned from recess scowling. Josie, always magnanimous, greeted him as if nothing had happened while Eli smiled smugly by her side. The two boys competition became a constant drama that required all of their attention and strategic intelligence, and it was played out throughout the day in every possible context—from music class to gym to a science lesson. But Eli was still coming out short.

Eli's main problem in this struggle was that Andrew was very powerful in the class, and he lost no opportunity to make sure Eli looked bad in public. Andrew used sharing time and silent reading to humiliate Eli by focusing undue attention on his efforts, and if *he* didn't make remarks or feign disinterest in Eli's stories, his friends Charles and Michael did it for him. One day, for example, Eli asked Andrew if he could continue Andrew's fake story from a few days before; this was during a period when the children added on to their friends' stories for weeks at a time. Andrew, who was sitting up front by the chair, cheerfully gave Eli his permission, but as Eli began to expand the story and was really amusing the class, I heard Michael and Charles in the background, saying, "Ha, ha, I forgot to laugh," over and over again until one of the girls turned around and ordered them to be quiet.

A few weeks later, Eli asked to use Andrew's story again, but this time Andrew said he wouldn't let him use it (even though this request had never been turned down by any other child). Eli, clearly insulted and hurt as he sat in the chair in front of his classmates, became extremely upset and began to cry, then punched Daniel, who was sitting right in front of him. Daniel, who had been sitting quietly waiting for Eli's story, was completely surprised by this attack, but we managed to subdue him before he swung back. After Eli realized that Daniel had only been smiling in anticipation of his story, not in amusement at his humiliation, he apologized, dried his tears, and went on to tell his own story.

THE DYNAMICS OF POWER AGAIN

Eli, whose skin was not black, experienced much the same kind of scrutiny for most of the year that Germaine had come under late in the year when he shifted the balance of power. But for Eli that kind of scrutiny made him more stubborn, rather than compensatory. He refused to compromise his goals in the chair, at silent reading, during science talks, or on the playground, and often fiercely confronted any of the boys who were excluding him. His pride and vulnerability, though, only emphasized how marginalized he was: if he couldn't be friends with the powerful boys and Josie, he wanted no friends at all; if he couldn't sit at the same table as Andrew or Josie, he would sit alone; if he couldn't play with Josie or Andrew after school, he would spend the afternoon alone.

Then sadly, after a few months, Eli began to take the bad boys' attitude and style and use it to intimidate other vulnerable children. Sometimes his actions were very low key, taking the form of sarcasm that confused the less verbal students. His tone was understood, but the readjustments of power that would have happened for the bad boys did not occur because the other children were not wary of Eli's authority. By the end of the year, as Eli became increasingly more frustrated with his treatment and exclusion by the very children he admired so much, he turned his attention to children outside of class.

One day in late May, Eli and the other boys were sitting at the lunch table when Anthony, an African-American boy from a special education class, came over to join them for lunch as he did every day and put his lunch down at the last empty space at the table.

"*You* can't sit there." Eli said, sarcastically, "that is a reserved seat," and he smiled broadly at the other boys.

"Yeah," added Phillip, "you can't sit here."

Anthony left to find his teacher to help him negotiate the situation. Eli got out of his seat, pushed Anthony's lunch bag into the middle of the table, and sat back down. Anthony returned with the teacher, noticed where his lunch bag was, and, as Michael later told me, "I saw a tear, just one big tear, trickling down his cheek." At that point the teacher realized what had happened, and, after delivering a lecture to all the boys, took Anthony away to eat with her.

As they left, Phillip said, "Hooray, Anthony's leaving." Eli smiled and nodded approvingly, as if he were taking a bow. All the boys at the table, which included all the boys in my class, looked away and were silent.

When I was told about the incident later by the teacher and then talked to the boys as a group, it was clear that, except for Phillip and Eli, they had been embarrassed by the incident but had chosen not to intervene. Michael, especially, understood exactly the implications of what had happened. When I asked the group of boys how Anthony must have felt, Michael said, "I think he probably felt like we were calling him the 'N' word."

Phillip said, "What does that mean, the 'N' word?"

"It means," replied Michael in a whisper, "nigger."

All of a sudden, Germaine, who hadn't appeared to have been listening to this exchange, jumped like he'd been shot, rose to his knees, and said, with an unusually aggressive tone, "What did you say?"

"The 'N' word means "nigger," and that's what I think Anthony felt like, but I don't like to say that word."

Germaine, as always, did not visibly respond, and sat back down.

Looking at Race

This incident provides, I think, a clear example of how convoluted the issue of race is among children. If we begin with Michael's analysis of what Eli's action meant symbolically, it is clear that he understood that the incident had racist overtones. But when Phillip, who was Chinese, asked what the "N" word meant, it is clear that many of those implications were beyond his understanding. In fact, in this situation Phillip was very much like Eli, but without the social consciousness of being disempowered. Phillip was Chinese, but also a first-generation American, born and raised in this country. He, like Germaine, did not understand all the social dynamics of the classroom; he rarely participated in the dramas and never initiated any of his own. In the social hierarchy Phillip was a loner and was almost always outside the games and dramas of the other children, usually because he did not understand how to participate in them. Thus when he joined Eli in this particular incident he did not have a complete understanding of the rules he was breaking or the implications of his act. Rather, he was joining in on the exclusion of another child, something that happened to him frequently.

In essence, Phillip knew he was often excluded by other children, did not know why, and happily participated in excluding another outsider.

When, however, Germaine heard Michael say the word "nigger," he immediately came to life. He knew the use of the that term was completely unacceptable; earlier in the year he had related a story to me about what he would do to anyone who called him a nigger. But Germaine, also at the table, had not defended Anthony's right to be there! His behavior led me to believe that he did not identify Anthony's exclusion by Eli as being in any way like his own experience. I don't believe he understood Michael's point, either.

But from my perspective, Michael's point was the only conclusion one could draw. Eli, who had been hurt so many times, chose as his target, as his unwilling co-actor in this event, an African-American child, understanding as he did so that Anthony was a vulnerable outsider and therefore ought to be a good target. Eli could spot the one child who was of lower status than himself and who was, therefore, safe to intimidate. Unfortunately, however, Eli (like Andrew in his question to Germaine in Chapter 3) had crossed a taboo boundary. None of the boys, including the bad boys, chose to participate in the drama. Eli received no support or approval from the children he sought to impress, and he gained no points in the game. Nevertheless, a week later, he tried again.

At recess Eli and his sometimes friends were playing on the swings when an African-American girl in the fifth grade came over to swing. As she went to sit in the empty swing next to Eli, he put his hand on the chain so she couldn't use it and told her the swing wasn't for her to use. She had a few words with him, then left and reported the incident to her teacher. Unlike Phillip or Germaine, she knew what Eli's exclusion implied. When I sat down with Eli and confronted him about the incident, reminding him of what he had done to Anthony a week earlier, he was casual, almost proud of himself. "Why," I asked, "would you want to hurt people who have never done anything to you?"

"Because," he replied with a smile, "other people hurt me over and over again. So I want to hurt other people."

"But why do you choose these particular children? They are both African-American children you hardly even know."

"Because they can't hurt me back."

I think his answer was absolutely right. Eli knew that these children really had very little recourse once he had offended them. They could tell a teacher and make him apologize, but they couldn't take away the feeling of superiority and power he experienced when he excluded them. They also couldn't hurt him from within the world of the classroom. And in fact, they always acted predictably when he excluded them. They went away and sought help from an adult, rather than precipitating a power struggle within the immediate moment of the interaction. For me, Eli's actions and the ways that they embodied his experience of the public world added another twist to the convoluted dynamics of power and race as children understand and perform them.

His actions, though, revealed a clear pattern of cause and effect. If anything, Eli, who seemed to be displaying openly racist behaviors, was operating in a much more simplistic and transparent fashion than were his more powerful classmates. As a result, the adults in his life could uncover his motives and work with them much more easily than we could understand and deal with those of the bad boys, and perhaps that was what he wanted. While Eli's intentions and motives were obvious to himself and everyone else, the intentions and motives of the bad boys were, I believe, as unknown to themselves as they were to me. Thus their efforts to disempower others were potentially more damaging to themselves and the other children, and made adult efforts to understand and assist them much more difficult.

There is, however, another side to this argument: *the bad boys never to my knowledge initiated an event focused on social power with children from outside the class.* Their primary focus in their social machinations was to maintain status, not to hurt indiscriminately. Does that make any sense? Can we say there is a difference between their actions and those of Eli? Their efforts, I think, were directed at dynamic social outcomes that would shape the climate of the class. It was social control that motivated them. Eli, on the other hand, had no real social power, and so initiated his events with outsiders. He would not risk losing membership in the classroom community by orchestrating conflict with children whom he wanted to be his friends. It was precisely his feeling of lack of control and an absence of personal power that motivated him to act. Thus his inability to control the dynamics of his social relationships prompted him to hurt innocent children who had no understanding of his motives. It looks like racism because both his victims were African American, but it's not quite that. It's rather a representation of one child's very correct perception of how the social hierarchy in our society works.

We can't absolutely name Eli's behavior as racist, but we can say that he understood some of the nuances of racism in society at large. And if we were to draw a diagram of how Eli's performance developed, that diagram would have to include Andrew, Josie, Michael, and Charles, and, in fact, every child who witnessed or participated in Eli's actions of exclusion as co-actors. The construction of this performance of exclusion involved many voluntary and involuntary players and had a history we can trace. There were players who disempowered Eli for purposes of maintaining their own social power; players, like Josie, who tried to maintain a middle ground but only exacerbated the struggle; players, like Phillip, who egged Eli on; players, like the boys in my class, who by not objecting, formed a cohort of excluders; and there were the reluctant co-actors, like Anthony, who just happened to enter the drama at a particular moment in time.

CHAPTER 10

Girls in Public

Field Notes: November

This year the emerging characteristic of my class is that the boys have all the answers, and the girls (with a few exceptions) have none. This is most clear when we are having whole class activities or discussions. No matter how long we wait, the girls, unless compelled, are silent and offer no ideas. In science talk, only two contribute. Others must be directly asked to say a few words. Are they really silent? Are they intimidated? I think the silence is self-imposed. When I asked Alexis why she was so quiet, she said she was "afraid of Daniel" (Daniel? Good heavens, he is not what I'd call intimidating) "because one time he wasn't nice in kindergarten." One time? How many girls do I have? Eleven. Four Japanese (they have an excuse to be quiet); two talkers; Mia and Josie; and five silent ones, Rachel, Alexis, Dierdre, Latia, and Jennifer, who has a language disability.

Silence and no answers: that was the essence of the girls in my all second-grade class that I had identified by mid-November. Obviously I was disturbed about it—and puzzled, because there was not any tangible pressure for students to be that way in my class, at least that I could perceive in my observations. It wasn't that the girls weren't emotionally or intellectually present; it was more that they were unable to participate in the intellectual exchanges of our day. I could tell by the ways that they hovered about me before each teaching sequence, rushed to science talks, and arranged themselves on the floor at sharing time for the best view, that they desired to be involved in the kinds of exchanges we had every day. Yet they were unable to put their feet in the water, as it were, to jump off the dock, swim straight out, away from shore, and trust that they would be safe and successful.

In the four years in which I did this research, I tried to identify the character of the girls in their public dealings. I looked at sharing time, science talks, and classroom teaching/learning interactions in different kinds of groups. What I found uniformly was this: in their first year with me, the girls most commonly exhibited a reluctance to "perform" in public, either in the sense of engaging in a social performance, or in a learning performance that took place in front of others. In some cases—for example, those with Rachel, and some I will describe later in this chapter— a few girls would not participate even in small group learning events. My notes conveyed the feeling that they were mired in a pit of longing and self-doubt: there was a desire to learn and be taught, but a fear of failure.

PUBLIC VERSUS PRIVATE

I have since come to see this combination of desire and fear as a defining characteristic of many of the girls' *public* interactions in the classroom. I don't believe it is a characteristic that would describe their private interactions, based on my observations of them on the playground and in same-sex play and work groups. In those cases, the girls were outspoken, animated, direct, cooperative, and task oriented. They showed a great deal of visible emotion, used dramatic strategies to make their points, and did not accept interference in their affairs by outsiders. For example, one day in winter, during a class study of how the earliest migrations to the Americas might have taken place, I asked the children to role play a mammoth hunt. Earlier, we had enacted carrying heavy burdens across snow and ice and had practiced throwing imaginary spears and rocks to kill game. I had decided to put the children in same-sex groups particularly to prevent the boys from dominating the planning and leading of a hunt scenario.

As the children broke into groups, the girls immediately organized themselves to make up a hypothetical story and a plan for the hunt, taking the task very seriously. Alexis proposed a scenario in which they'd divert the attention of an old bull and then entrap it. This idea was discussed and modified by the group. In the course of the discussion, the girls went to a chalkboard, picked up a piece of chalk, then drew a map on the floor indicating where the bull was, where they were, where they wanted the bull to be, and where each hunter would position herself. The map showed a hypothetical topography for the area they were in, including river, valley, and hills. Their plan was to find the mammoth herd, wait until the bull was feeding away from the herd, and then distract it by running across its path, thus luring it away from the herd and drawing it into a trap.

The girls organized parts quite quickly: They would gather the food together and put it in a place where they anticipated the bull would wander, and Dierdre would create the distraction that would lure the bull. Certain girls volunteered to be those who would drive the bull into the trap; others said they would be waiting in ambush.

They rehearsed, played out the scene as they had planned it, regrouped and talked about what didn't work, and revised their plans. Dierdre went back to the map and added to it, drawing arrows to show which way the bull would come, where she would be, which direction she would go in, and where the hunters should stand. They performed the drama again, and then once more, each time with more precision and always with great seriousness. After thirty minutes, they were satisfied with their plan and asked to show it to the boys. (It is interesting to note that while the girls were proceeding with such seriousness, order, and creativity, the boys were mired in arguing over who would be the leader. I saw that Andrew, Michael, and Eli all wanted to be in charge and were arguing viciously about who would do the best job. They were unable to compromise on any issue because each wanted to play the most important roles, plan the hunt, and tell the other boys what to do. Charles, who loved drama more than any other part of the school day, was vainly trying to convince the three to cooperate so they could get on with the performance. The rest of the boys sat glumly to the side of the arguing three, passively waiting for them to resolve their differences. By the time the session was finished, the boys had not resolved their disagreements, even with the assistance of both me and my intern.)

The behavior observed in the private all-girl work group, however, was never typical of their public work in mixed-sex groups. In public, the girls were soft spoken or silent, showed very little emotion, did not spontaneously initiate ideas or assume responsibility for planning, used indirect means to signal that they needed help in the large group, waited until the group dispersed to ask questions, and very rarely said what they needed without a direct request from me or from another child. This passive demeanor was the usual presentation I encountered in my *first* year with girls. By the second year, in most girls these traits had disappeared. (I will return to that point later in the chapter.)

The Strategy of Concealment

Because of the fact that girls conceal themselves in public, it is very hard for teachers to know what they are thinking, what they believe, and what they do and don't understand. If they seem to fade into the background in most classrooms, I believe that that strategy for becoming less visible is not so much a function of the overt social pressure of boys and lack of attention from the teacher as it is a way of coping with their *awareness of the presence of boys* as an audience. Within that public context, any occasion of uncertainty or risk results in the strategy of concealment. In contrast, however, many boys see that kind of risk and uncertainty as stimulating. Poor things, they also see the possibility of doing back flips off of a high concrete wall as equally risky, and therefore stimulating. Many girls, however, have a more calculating attitude toward personal display in public. They do not throw themselves off high walls or into the middle of a new classroom activity, but rather wait and watch, and, if possible, stay out of the center of any uncomfortable interaction. The classroom, a hotbed of risk and discomfort, and therefore metaphorically like a high concrete wall from which they must jump, immediately provides them with an untenable position. They come to school to fit in and be good, but they find themselves surrounded by a much more complex academic and social milieu than they've experienced anywhere. "Being good" implies more than just behaving; it implies understanding what the teacher is teaching without causing a disruption in the flow of the instruction, and thereby also pleasing the teacher. Most girls, then, work to fit in and be good, but also to appear competent; and they achieve this goal by keeping a very low profile, which helps them stay at a particular level of anonymity so as to not be singled out for too much attention from either teacher or peers.

"Being good" does not get you social power, but it does get you lots of support and admiration from your (usually) female teacher. (We can harken back here to Chapter 2, when I described my longing for calm and neural integration.) I guess what I'm doing here is taking the notion that girls are suppressed and thereby "shortchanged" by schools, and turning it around a bit to say that some girls, in my experience, come into school as 6-year-olds with a coping mechanism that relies on taking a safe road. That safe road shortchanges them just as Rachel's silence shortchanged her, the bad boys' words and desires to be powerful shortchanged them, and Dierdre's posing shortchanged her. As their teacher, I do not find it helpful to try and figure out how their desire to take the safe road came about. Nor is it helpful to see myself as the sole agent of each of these limiting performances. Rather, it is more useful to build a description of the safe road when it is employed in the classroom and to determine in what ways, as a co-actor, I sometimes unwittingly further their journey down the safe road. In this way I can work to mitigate the effects of the performances, and also and most important, determine how best to teach these girls so that the safe road is not as attractive.

THE SAFE ROAD

It's important here to take a look at how the safe road plays itself out in a primary classroom. We will begin with girls we haven't met yet because they did their best to stay out of confusing or difficult social situations and maintained very low profiles for most of the school year. Their absence from many of the events I've described in this book indicate to what extent they succeeded in concealing themselves from my observations.

Latia and Alexis, two quite different girls from contrasting backgrounds, both of whom came to me as second graders, will help me illustrate the kind of protective barrier that is set up by girls. Latia was African American and from a family of five children: one older sister, two older brothers, and a younger sister. I had taught both of her older brothers and knew Latia even before she entered kindergarten at our school. Her mother was finishing her college degree and raising the children by herself. Alexis was Caucasian, and an only child. Her parents were both professionals and academics.

Latia

My first observation of Latia comes from the first week of school in early September. My field notes record the following:

> Latia was reserved and a loner all day. She didn't initiate conversations, except with Flutterbutter and Sarah, our cockatiels. She did talk to me because I am "family," having taught her two brothers. (Her brother John delivered her to me on opening day with the words, "Look, Latia, here's Karen. She'll take care of you, just like she did us, so you don't need to worry about a thing.") Today, during the only time in which we had an assigned task, which was to draw a picture about something she did this summer, Latia wouldn't participate. Cindy [my intern] reports that when she tried to assist Latia in getting started, she didn't seem able to talk about her ideas and was "inside of herself." When I questioned Latia at the end of the day about her decision not to do the summer picture, she was not able to articulate what the problem had been for her. She told me that she could draw, but she couldn't "do it right," pointing to erasures on her paper.

Latia continued to be almost paralyzed by any activities that required her to be publicly competent at any level. Usually the activities required no particular show of new learning, but were going to result in some kind of display either for myself or for the class. For example, the following scenario developed when I asked the children to pick a book of their choice and read part of it.

Field Notes: September

> Latia sits herself in a chair and eats her snack, making no move to select a book or see me. I call her over and seat her next to me while a Japanese child struggles to read a simple book in English. Latia registers no emotion on her face. When I ask if she'll look at the same book for me and try to read a little of it, she says *nothing*, won't look or speak or move. I spend several minutes speaking quietly, cajoling, using simple logic as to why I want her to read the pages, but to no effect. So, twenty minutes later, after everyone else has gone to lunch, Latia and I still sit side by side silently. I explain to her again how important it is for me to know what she can and can't do, so that I can teach her. I also explain that neither of us is moving until she reads a little bit to me. Finally she says she'll try, and a single tear rolls down her cheek. She does just fine. When I ask her why she wouldn't try, she says, "I'm scared."
>   "Scared of what?" I ask. She can't say.

That conversation represented a turning point with Latia and me, but only within our private interactions. In other instructional times with the whole group, she remained silent, almost enclosed. My notes record that Latia did not share in front of the whole class until late October, and when she did her voice was so soft none of us could hear her. By late November, Latia shared regularly, and with pleasure, but the pattern was that she required other children's questions and comments to bring her out. Giving out information, even about things she was familiar with, was not comfortable for her. For example, in early December, Latia shared a Play-a-Tune book. She got into the chair and said, "This is my Play-a-Tune book. Questions or comments." She didn't explain the book or play it. Then Alexis asked her to play something. She shook her head no, but pushed the book toward Alexis so that she could press a key, and Alexis did. The children oohed and ahhed and commented among themselves. At that point Cindy asked if each key played a different note, and Latia played the keys to show that they did. Why, I wondered, wouldn't she play a key to respond to Alexis's question, but then, after she saw the positive reaction, play for us?

A week later, when Latia shared a home computer, we made a small advance. "This is my home computer," Latia said. "It has a lot of games. Questions or comments." She didn't take the computer out of the box for us to see it, so Cindy asked her if she could, and she did reluctantly. A child asked if she could tell us the name of one game. She was silent. I prompted her again to tell us just one. "I don't know," she said, "I'm not sure." I pointed out to her that that was a good answer for a hard question. From that point on she used it frequently instead of responding to difficult questions with silence.

For Latia, any risky situation, even if she had encountered it before in a different context, would prompt avoidance through either silence or resistance. It took her three months for her first try at reading the daily schedule for the class, something every other child in the class had done routinely since September. That event took place only after tremendous coaxing and coaching from Cindy and me, including a rehearsal the day before and that morning before school. What was traumatic for her was not, in fact, the act of reading the chart, because she had seen that being done over and over again each morning by other children. The chart format and procedure remained fairly consistent. The trauma, I think, came from the position of being in front of the class and having the remote possiblity of faltering or missing a word. I had observed Latia reading the schedule on different occasions during the day when no one was looking, and reading it competently. But the act, the performance, the attention of the audience terrified her. My notes record her first attempt.

Field Notes: October

> Latia was quite excited yesterday because she had made a decision, with Cindy's and my help, that she would try to read the schedule today for the first time. But when she stands up to do it, she can't and starts to cry. Cindy is right next to her and is very solicitous, speaking softly to her, but this only seems to make Latia cry more. (Because she is disappointing Cindy? I, however, am very impatient with her, and say so. I have no pity.) Finally, because Latia seems absolutely paralyzed by fear, I ask if any of the children will help her. Latia turns to look at the class, and almost every single hand goes up in the air. I can see her surprise—her mouth about drops open and she forgets to cry. She immediately agrees that she'll try with a friend to help, and she chooses Dierdre to assist her, then reads the schedule with no problem.

Alexis

In looking back on my notes, I find it is interesting that Alexis shared for the first time on the same day as Latia. Her mother and father had been concerned, as had Latia's mother, that she hadn't shared, had spent several days persuading her that it wouldn't be as painful as she'd imagined, and then rehearsed with her what she might say. For her first time in the chair, Alexis brought in an avocado plant she had grown since first grade. She was tremendously apprehensive and almost rigid with fear when she got in the chair. After a few minutes, however, she relaxed when she saw that the children were quite interested in how she had grown the plant. Finally, as she went to get out of the chair, she caught herself, sat back down abruptly, and said, "Oh, I forgot something I wanted to say . . . can you guess how the leaves got this way?" and she pointed to a leaf with a small hole in it.

On her second sharing, three weeks later (children have the option to share once a week, always on the same day), Alexis was tense again, but got in the chair to share some paper she had made at an afterschool program. She said, "This is paper. I made it at LEDP (the program). Questions or comments." Like Latia, Alexis was reluctant to give information in front of the class, but in response to the question "How did you make it?" she gave a long and detailed response that showed how much she had learned in the papermaking process. Once again, by the end of her sharing she was visibly relaxed: her feet were perched up on the chair rail, and she was smiling and using a conversational tone. When Germaine distracted her with a sudden noise, she stopped and said, "Would you please stop that?" Germaine was rather surprised at the authoritative tone she used (as was I), and he stopped. Alexis continued taking questions and comments. Then she stopped again and said, "Oh, I meant to add this for Josie . . ." and added a comment about the screen that related to Josie's earlier question. Watching her, and then Latia, who followed, I wrote:

> Alexis is clearly enjoying herself at this point. The children are very respectful and responsive to her. Latia is also sharing regularly now and is quite assertive in making sure the class is well behaved during her time in the chair, although she and Alexis do require questions and comments to bring them out. Is this a "girl" thing, part of the protocol that girls see as socially responsible? That is, you don't just get up in the chair and ramble on, pretending you know everything. That's egotistical, and most of us are impatient with that kind of person. These girls seem to think this and prefer to create a kind of *conversation* about what they are showing. It's not a display, it's a dialogue which they are in charge of (as they both demonstrate so aptly).

However, although Alexis did develop a comfortable strategy for handling sharing, she retained a quiet, impassive approach to every other public teaching and learning occasion. As with Latia, my observations of Alexis doing the morning schedule helped me see her dilemma as a public person.

Field Notes: November 30

> Alexis is doing the chart this morning. When she comes to the word "Jour_ _ _s" (Journals), which has been left partially blank for her to complete the spelling, she fills in the N, then stands looking at Cindy, completely silent (unwilling to try it?). Cindy encourages her, but she's not having any of it. Finally, after quite a wait, she turns to the class and signals she needs help by standing and looking at them. They take the cue, and many hands go up. (Are we talking pride here? She wasn't about to be embarrassed. She'll make mistakes privately, but not in public.)

During science talks Alexis was silent until late spring (as was Latia), and then when she spoke it was clear from her voice that she was very nervous. She would make an effort, though, because she wanted to *please me.* Both she and Latia understood from our private conversations that talking in science talks, contributing to discussions about books, and asking for help when they needed it were things I wanted them to try to do. So they both tried, but the efforts clearly took a lot out of them.

Coping With Uncertainty

There were small gains, though. Latia had a habit (which I'd heard about when she was in kindergarten and first grade, and which I saw in full force in my classroom) of doing what I came to call "shutting down" whenever she encountered a new instructional expectation. For example, if I said, "I'd like you to make a list of things that crawl," Latia would drop any expression from her face, pull her legs into her body, if she was sitting on the rug, wrap her arms around them, and become immobile. When I first saw this, I interpreted it as defiance. Later I saw a pattern in when it occurred and realized it was a behavior triggered by new expectations: performance expectations. It came to signal: "I'm scared." Throughout the year Cindy and I treated the response as a signal of fear and used the occasion to carefully reassure her of her competence and to break down the steps she needed to follow until she realized the task was not insurmountable. Latia became less immobilized by her fear but was unable to overcome the immediate reaction until finally, in late April, she made a simple breakthrough.

The class had been reading poems about spring, and on this particular day we read a poem listing things we could do in spring. Together we wrote our own poem, with each child developing his or her own line, which I wrote on a large chart. Latia did this part of the task with no problem, since writing a group poem was something we had done for several months, and she had learned that her composing would be respected by the other children. This time, however, I explained that we were going to take our poem and create a large mural which would illustrate each line. I passed out strips of paper to the children and asked them to copy their line onto the paper strip so that we could attach it to the mural later when it was completed. As the children dispersed, Latia came up, cheerfully took her paper strip, and strolled away, grabbing a pencil. I noticed that she hadn't had the characteristic "shutdown" in the face of this new activity but didn't think much about it. About 10 minutes later, as I was sitting at a table working with a child, Latia came up to me, excused herself, and asked if I could explain the assignment again, 'because I don't really get it." Again I was surprised, because Latia had rarely, if ever, asked directly for my help, choosing rather to sit silent and inactive and wait for me to offer it, or simply to shut down. I reexplained the task, and she thanked me quite cheerfully and went back to her seat. Five minutes later she returned, pulled up a chair, and said, "Karen, I still don't get it. Could you show me how it should look to be right," I took a strip that another child had just finished and showed it to her.

"Oh," she said, "that's what I thought," and she went off to complete the assignment.

For me this was a real achievement, and it underscored the kind of change that Latia had to make to begin moving off the safe road. To an observer, it might seem like a trivial exchange, but in the context of our shared experience for over seven months, Latia was finally able to see past her fear of "not doing it right," *and to ask for help*. To some, the act of asking for help in front of others is not at all difficult. For Latia, Alexis, Dierdre, Rachel, and many young girls in classrooms, asking for help is very, very hard. It requires them to acknowledge in public that they may not be competent. Asking other kinds of questions is also hard because on the same level it implies that the child does not know something or does not fully understand the assignment or the subject matter. Little girls are very proud, much more proud than most little boys, who have no qualms about asking for help, In fact, most boys demand help, saying they don't understand something, even going so far as saying that something is not very interesting. For these little girls, such a statement would be unthinkable, and asking anything in front of others is risky.

THE SECOND YEAR

Unfortunately, I did not have a second year with Alexis and Latia, although for both of them the transformation from September to June was striking.

I believe that change came as a result of my discomfort with their silence, and that my discomfort, in turn, was fueled by my process as a teacher researcher interested in gender. Their progress in moving into the public world, though, was not guaranteed to hold over with a new teacher and a newly composed class of peers. However, for those girls I have for two years, the kinds of changes Alexis and Latia experienced are confirmed in their second year. Not only am I viewed as a safe and trustworthy individual, but so are their classmates. The mingling of fear of failure with the desire to participate is mitigated by their realization that in order to belong to a classroom community they have to participate fully, and further, that participation is much more personally rewarding, in spite of its perceived dangers, than the safety of concealment.

Rachel, for example, having emerged from her silence in first grade, became much more able in her second year to ask for help, to share her ideas, and even to contradict powerful boys in science talks. Ellen, whom we saw in Chapter 7 as a second grader, was quite timid and shy as a first grader but moved into a much more experimental mode in second grade, where the safe road for her was clearly not the interesting road. As for Dierdre, she retained her public reserve unless she was clearly pushed by me to give it up, and then she would do so only briefly. Dierdre, however, had other dynamics working for her which complicated her public interactions (see Chapter 5). For most girls who are quiet, passive, and "shy," two years with a teacher and a class that work at being a community of learners is a means to achieving full participation and agency in the classroom. In fact, as we have seen, two years holds that potential for boys and girls alike, freeing them to work through many ways of being in the classroom both as a friend and as a student.

GIRLS WHO DON'T TAKE THE SAFE ROAD

Sharing Time: November 4

> Mia is preparing to share a new Polly Pocket. As she sits in the chair and opens the toy, the boys start to groan and gesture to each other that it's disgusting by sticking their fingers down their throat. Mia closes the Polly Pocket and stares grimly at the crowd. Silence falls, and she proceeds to give the boys a mini lecture on how what they're doing makes her feel sad and embarrassed, and it's not fair, and she might as well not share at all, if that's how they'll act. The boys are chastened and look down at their hands, trying to avoid her defiant stare. Mia proceeds with her sharing and the boys actually let themselves enjoy it, participating enthusiastically.

Like Latia and Alexis, Mia entered our class in second grade. Unlike her two friends, however, Mia was intrepid in the face of new and unexpected classroom events. Why she was able to show such daring is unclear. Her family background, like Latia's and Alexis's, reveals little in contrast to that of other children: Mia was Caucasian, the first of two girls. Both her parents were professionals. For my purposes as a teacher, that is the kind of information I have to work with, and so for the purposes of understanding Mia's different way of interacting in the classroom, I can really only provide an account of her public style.

The sharing time episode described above catches the flavor of Mia's interactions with the class. It quickly became apparent when she joined us in September that Mia's thoughts and feelings would never be concealed at her own expense. When faced with difficulty or ambiguity, Mia would not, as most of her girl friends might, assume a position of impassivity and inaction, but would rather forge ahead into the center of a situation. Her approach, though, does not have the flavor of, for example, Tony or Andrew's plotting, or the "hurtling" bravado of other little boys; it was spontaneous, but completely rooted in the present tense and completely directed at her *being* competent. There was no desire to obscure what she didn't know, no artifice, no attempt to control others, no orchestrating of conflict as we've seen in other chapters. Mia was spontaneous and always direct, and if she didn't understand something, she would ask me or others to help her figure it out. My notes record her questioning other children's intentions, asking me questions when she didn't understand something, thinking out loud even when her thoughts were not organized, engaging gamely in performances orchestrated by the boys (rather than retreating into silence), asking directly to be included in the fake stories told by the boys (something only she and Josie, out of all the girls, did), and even telling fake stories of boy/girl conflict in which the girls were triumphant over the boys.

Mia would often provide the impetus for girls and boys to try out new behaviors, simply through her own willingness to take risks in public. She was proud to be feminine and publicly declared that through her stories and sharing. In other classroom events she was quite intrepid, contributing ideas, taking chances, proposing theories, and asking questions of other children when she didn't understand their ideas. In friendships, in direct contrast to her friends, Mia showed the same traits. For example, over a period of a month one fall, I followed the progress of a friendship group that included Rachel, Alexis, Mia, and Dierdre. These girls were constantly struggling to find a way to play together without conflict. They would return from recess each day subdued by the difficulties they'd had at lunch recess. Usually without fail Mia would approach me and tell, with great hystrionics, the saga of that recess, complete with a flinging of arms, huffing, pointing, and occasionally tears, but always concluding with a huge sigh and a sulk. Sometimes the arguments they'd had would break out anew as they entered the classroom, when Mia would wait for the other girls and confront them as they walked up the steps. Generally the other three were tongue tied, able only to agree mutely that they had a very big problem, but unable to talk about what it was.

One day, after yet another incident, I got the girls together and asked them what was going on, why they couldn't play in fours instead of twos. Alexis was livid that day because Dierdre and Rachel wouldn't play with Mia and her. Rachel explained that one day she'd played with Dierdre, and the next day she'd played with Alexis, and the next day she'd played with Mia. As Rachel said this, Mia interrupted. "But why, why not all of us? Boys can do it!" Rachel continued to explain that when they played together they always had a big fight, and that her only way to manage that was to either go "hide behind a tree" (a very Rachelian solution), or play with one friend each day, and no more. That declaration left Mia speechless, and the discussion ended without a resolution.

Two weeks later, as the battles continued, I suggested that the four try once again to talk about their problem. Once again the scenario unfolded of Alexis and Mia confronting Rachel and Dierdre about excluding them. About five minutes into the discussion, Mia jumped up and said, "I know, let's have a kind of play so we can show you [meaning me] how this works out over and over again." Alexis immediately agreed, and Rachel and Dierdre reluctantly said that would be okay. Mia conferred with Alexis and then assigned parts: Mia would be Dierdre, and Dierdre would be Mia; Alexis would be Rachel, and Rachel would have to be Alexis. In fact, what unfolded was a psychodrama in which Mia and Alexis acted every part, playing both themselves and the other two girls. Dierdre and Rachel stood by quietly and watched, each unable to take on the role of the other.

PUBLIC GIRLS AND THE OTHER

Sharing Time: May 11

GERMAINE (telling a true story about when he took karate): Once when I was at karate, my teacher did a back flip. He teached us how to do it. Then, when we knew how to do it, it was kind of hard. We had to do three cartwheels to do it. And when it was over, I asked him, could I pass? And he tested me. And I passed. Questions or comments?
ELI: What do you mean by "passed"?
GERMAINE: I passed the test: two stripes.

CHARLES: What belt are you?

GERMAINE: We don't have belts.

MIA: In kindergarten, Rachel and me were the only two girls in karate. Then we quit because we were embarrassed.

GERMAINE: Sometimes they let me be in the grownup class.

MIA: I think we should give Germaine a hand 'cause he passed his test. (The class claps right away. Germaine, normally completely impassive, reacts by a slight shifting of his eyebrows. It's very subtle, almost like an involuntary reaction of surprise and pleasure to Mia's suggestion and the class's response. This is as close as he gets to registering emotion, and it's a strong one, I think.)

That Mia was daring and straightforward in her interpersonal dealings was clear for everyone who knew her. The consequences of her daring, though, were not rejection or isolation in the class, but the achievement of a certain kind of clout and deep loyalty from children like Germaine. She was often heard celebrating other children's achievements: persuading Rachel (an aspiring chef) to share the biscuits they'd made the night before "just from whatever we found!"; prompting a silent Dierdre to speak in science talks by pointing out how much Dierdre knew about science; praising Nathaniel for his daily improvement as a storyteller ("You are almost always funny, and you just make me laugh"), and in all these cases seeming to understand both the desires of other girls and the less confident boys to be seen and heard, *respectfully*, by others. She wanted others to get the kind of respect that she'd demanded earlier in the year for herself.

A description of Mia also draws attention to her desire *to be seen* and to be a public person. Her approach to the classroom community offers a vivid contrast to the efforts of other girls to efface themselves. During the four years in which I was following the social relations of three classes of these children, I can recall only three other girls who were like Mia in their comfort in the public sphere: Shelley (who does not appear in this book), Ellen, and Josie. By example, these girls offered an alternative way of being in the classroom and a unique perspective on what the social work of childhood ought to be. It was one that did not recognize the boundaries that gender seemed to impose on both girls and boys, and, as they crossed over the borders, other children watched and eventually followed, trying on new characters and experimenting with new kinds of public selves.

Field Notes: May 17

It is late in the day and we are singing. I ask if anyone has a request, or a song they'd like to teach us. Alexis, Dierdre, and Latia immediately jump up and signal that they do. "Well, it's not a song, really," says Alexis, "it's more like a song game." I suggest they go ahead, and call the children's attention to them, and then signal them to begin. It takes them a few minutes to get organized, but they finally arrange themselves and stand facing each other.

Down, down, baby,
Down by the rollercoaster.
Sweet, sweet baby, I don't want to let you go.
Shimmy, shimmy, cocoa puff, shimmy, shimmy whoo!
Shimmy, shimmy, cocoa puff, shimmy, shimmy, whoo!
Doctor, Doctor, sick in bed,
Called to the doctor and the doctor said,
"Let's get the rhythm of the head, ding-dong (bobbing head).
Let's get the rhythm of the head, ding-dong.
Let's get the rhythm of the feet (stamp feet twice).
Let's get the rhythm of the feet (stamp, stamp).
Let's get the rhythm of the Ho-ot Dog (swiveling hips)
Let's get the rhythm of the Ho-ot Dog.
Ding-dong, (stamp, stamp), Ho-ot Dog!
Ding-dong, (stamp, stamp), Ho-ot Dog!"

As they sing and do the game, which is really a hand-jive, the girls begin to smile and the boys giggle and cover their faces ("Oh, my God!"). When the girls are finished, Alexis says, "Now, we're going to teach it to everybody." "Oh, my God"s resound noisily all around, but the girls jump up and grab partners. I see pandemonium raising its ugly head, but then I hear Andrew's voice, "All right, I'll do it!" and he jumps up, dragging Josie with him. "Not me, no way!" says Michael, but boys are leaping up all around him and pairing off. Charles comes over, takes Michael's hands, and drags him out as Michael complains loudly. The girls explain that everyone should just watch them and try to follow. I am sitting in my chair with my mouth agape as the spectacle unfolds. Five minutes later they are going through the song for the third time and the boys, who have massive coordination problems, are singing loudly and ignoring the fact that they are just a few beats behind, doing the Ho-ot Dog hips just slightly after the words, but they are quite giddy with joy over the goofiness of it all. And so am I.

CHAPTER 11

Dreamin' of How It Could Be

TEACHER: Rachel, what are you doing when you're so quiet?

RACHEL: I'm dreamin', like, of how it could be, like, to be a horse, or Aladdin . . . on his carpet . . . or anything. Sometimes I play the anything game. In the game you can be anything you want, any character . . . and you can change whenever you want.

Conversation with Rachel: March 29

(Rachel, Daniel, and Dierdre are playing "horses" in the meeting area during an indoor recess. Rachel has one of her favorite books on horses resting on my chair. It is open to a particular page showing the different breeds. Since it is noon, I call the class to story, but these three continue to prance around the meeting area.)

TEACHER: Rachel, can you put the game to bed? (Rachel shrugs characteristically and smiles at me as she prances, then stops and walks over to the open book on my chair.)

RACHEL: I was being a piebald, my favorite.

TEACHER: I hate to interrupt, but it is time for story and the kids will need to sit here.

RACHEL: That's okay (to her friends, but audible to me). You can still play the game while the teacher's reading the story but you're just playing it in your head. (She looks at me and smiles, and I laugh.)

TEACHER: Rachel, I know that's what you've been doing for the past two years in story, 'cause I've watched you.

RACHEL: Yeah, but sometimes you can be playing the people *in the story* in your head. (I think Rachel is correcting me here. She's admitting her imagination but letting me know that sometimes she is imagining herself into the story I am reading.)

My work with Rachel, which began with her impenetrable silence, has enabled me to think about the question of what the silence itself might signal or embody for a child, and how that silence fits into the life of the classroom. This is a much more intangible and abstract train of thought than one which focuses on how her silence shuts out the life of the classroom, but it is one that I believe has important meanings for how we understand and observe a child's thinking about the world. The artifacts of this strand are particularly elusive. Outside the playtime of early childhood classrooms, it is particularly difficult to record real, unorchestrated examples of the rhythm and content of children's imaginal life. However, for two years Rachel allowed me to observe some of these "threads" of her silence (Merleau-Ponty, 1964), and those places where they intersected with the more mundane events of our classroom.

I now know, after finally breaking through her silence in our second year together, that Rachel had a vast panoply of worlds, real and imagined, that acted as both a refuge for her when the world of the classroom pushed too hard and as a bridge toward us when she began to be pulled into the center of classroom life. When Rachel spoke, the cadence and tone of her language seemed to reflect the life behind her silence. Her voice was extremely compelling, almost hypnotic. Because she said so little, her spoken words were more measured, more rich with meanings conveyed not by words, but by tone, physical intensity, and gaze. Further, the notion of silence as safety and power, or as protection and control, began to give ground to another interpretation: *silence as a container for a rich imaginal world.* I began to explore what happened for Rachel when she was silent, and because she no longer used her silence to avoid participation by masking it with a repertoire of avoidance gestures, I was able to speak with her about the silence and observe her in different classroom events fully immersed in her imaginal world.

Field Notes: October 20: 8:00 A.M.

> Rachel runs up to me when she enters the classroom with a long, gauzy opalescent scarf elegantly wrapped around her head and neck. She leans against me as I am writing to get my attention. As I look up, she whispers, "I wanted to wear this." She strokes the scarf against her cheek, sighs, and smiles. I am surprised by her image because she looks so much like an old-fashioned movie star, all glimmering and dewy eyed, and I tell her she looks beautiful. Then she becomes self-conscious, quickly takes it off, and crumples it in her hand as if to put it away. (I think she is suddenly struck by how public her imagination has become.) I say, "You look so beautiful, you should wear it all day. Don't take it off." She smiles and rewraps it around her head.

9:40 A.M.: In meeting, Rachel is sitting in the far corner of the meeting area, the scarf wrapped around her head and neck, then halfway around her waist, then tucked in her pants. She is absolutely still and silent, staring into space, her eyes wide and almost transparent, and she does look like a princess. I believe she is overtaken with the drama of the scarf.

9:45 A.M.: Rachel takes out her reading response journal and sits down next to Nick. The scarf is still wrapped elegantly around her head, neck, and waist. As she sits, Nick looks up, does a double take, looks up at me as I pass by, and pointing at Rachel, asks "What's that?" Rachel immediately stands up, loosens the scarf, and pulls it off, glancing at him self-consciously. She looks at me and shrugs, moving to take the scarf away. I am amazed at how Nick's small exclamation has crumbled her persona: she is almost apologetic, shrugging helplessly and looking as if she's been caught doing something wrong. I quietly exclaim, "But Rachel, Nick isn't saying it's bad. He's just noticing." "Yeah," Nick says, "it *really shines!*"

Rachel sits back down and rewraps the scarf, opens her journal, and begins to write. She is suddenly taller, and elegant, and peaceful.

10:30 A.M.: A parent who is a pediatrician is visiting the class to talk to us about one of our Science Talk questions. He has brought many books and posters and skillfully works with the children. Rachel is standing in the back corner, watching very carefully. Everyone else is sitting. She has her scarf tied in a huge, magnificent shimmering bow around her waist.

Now that I know her better, the question of what the silence covers emerges with more complexity. On one level, I could conclude, as I initially did, that it covered both fear of failure and embarassment, and was an effort to hold some power in what was a seriously assymetrical power relationship where other people held most of the chips. On another level, I believe her silence was filled with an imaginal world that is almost palpable to me now. One might say it is a world that is fiercely guarded by her silence, and rightly so. As Rachel began to speak more with me, I found myself almost irresistibly pulled into that world. She used so few words, and spoke slowly and intimately, pausing noticeably between thoughts, as if to consider each one again in silence. Her voice was quiet and rich, almost luxurious like new velvet, and when she said, "I'm, like, dreamin' of how it could be . . . ," I could feel the intensity and wonder of that dream; I remembered that I used to do that, too.

OBSERVING IMAGINATION

Field Notes From Science Talk: November 17

I had Rachel be a recorder for science talk today. I wanted to see whether, if she had a task, she could listen to what other children were saying and keep notes, rather than glazing over and checking out of the talk, as she usually does. I sat her in a chair (which she requested) with a clipboard, paper, and a pencil. The talk started and she began to write. But after a few phrases, she got "the look." Instead of looking and listening to the speakers, she let her eyes wander off, and she stared blankly at the bottom of the clipboard, her body listing to the side as she relaxed into her own place. When the talk finished 20 minutes later, she had written two lines: one from the first statement a child had made, and one from the last. Clearly for about 15 minutes she had zoned out. That was ten out of fifteen minutes she wasn't with us.

Rachel was certainly an extreme case. Her silence was very visible, and when it became less of a battleground for us, I could see the degree to which it transported her, and I knew that there was a fine balance to be cast between my needs as a teacher and Rachel's needs to build her own visions of the world. Soon I began to wonder about the other children and where that balance was for them. Most of them were not so obviously silent or so transported as Rachel, but I had no knowledge of what their "dreamin'" might be like. However, when I began to watch them, keeping this question in mind, I found that they constantly revealed that world to me and to each other in more public places. As I examined my observations of sharing time, recess, and their performances, I saw that the worlds they created were indeed imaginal worlds, filled with possibility. These worlds were not bounded by the legacies of the children's birth or culture. They were places where boundaries were consciously crossed and children could be "anything."

CROSSING BOUNDARIES

The Unicorn, by Ellen (Grade 1)

Once upon a time there was a unicorn. She was pretty, and she was wise, and she was kind. She was Queen of the Unicorns.

She had babies every year without mating. She had fun with her babies. They usually were girls. Boys were rare. That was why the Queen always could do it without a male.

Sometimes she was sad because she wasn't married, because none of the unicorns liked her. She offered them diamonds if they would marry her. But they did not want to. They hated her.

Sometimes she was glad she wasn't married. Because she would get mad at him a lot. She did not get mad very much. But she would get mad a lot.

She was sad, and unhappy, and lonely.

Then one day a strange unicorn came to the land. The Queen never saw him before. He was orange. She liked him and she wanted to marry him, and he wanted to marry her. They were friends for a long time. They wanted to be together all the time. They really wanted to get married.

So they got married a few years later. She never knew that he was a prince until they were alone in the tower.

They had children. They loved them. They loved each other. The end.

Sharing Time: April 13

Latia takes her turn to tell a fake story, and in it she turns Michael and Charles into a princess and a queen. The boys are obviously delighted with the idea and laugh and participate in the story. Then Daniel gets into the chair and says, "I'm going to share. I'm going to tell a fake story." (In the two years I've taught him, Daniel has never before told any.) He continues, "And it's got a title. It's called 'The Three Maids,' instead of 'The Three Musketeers.'" Daniel tells a story in which he, Michael, and Charles turn into maids. Although they are girls, they have adventures, as boys would, riding on rocket boosters or skateboarding, except that they are wearing dresses.

Daniel's sequence directly followed a long discussion after Latia's sharing in which the children described how Charles loved to dress up as a princess or a fairy at their parties. Mia related a story of the time when Charles came over to play: "Charles put on some fairy wings and a dress, and he told me to put on lipstick for him, and he was a fairy godmother. He was a good one, too." Mia added that Charles also had worn a tutu to one of her birthday parties when they were in kindergarten. (By the end of second grade, Charles was notorious for his hilarious costumes and his acting ability.) During this discussion, the children were very amused as they reminisced about Charles's love of girls' clothing and his ability to "be someone else." In this sharing session, Charles was quite comfortable with the remarks. In fact, he prides himself on his imitations of different stereotypes such as old ladies, officious men, and holiday figures like Santa Claus, or a wicked witch.

These two records of children's movement into imaginative work display their interest in crossing over the gender boundaries that society maintains for them. These are not unusual occurrences in the sense that by second grade, the children usually made the movement spontaneously, and with the kind of glee and glitter in the eye that usually occurs in adult comedy, when socially accepted norms are metaphorically dismantled. I have repeatedly seen second graders who have spent two years in close quarters that allow them to forge strong alliances from the perspectives of their own, rather than the school's, reality make a natural movement into this kind of parody. Usually the thrust of the parody is toward the caricature. For example, it is remarkable to see bad boys such as Michael and Charles—who depended for well over a year on asserting their power through social discourse that excluded and demeaned others—move into the use of comic performances in which they essentially emasculated themselves for the class's amusement.

As their teacher, I marveled that they had traveled beyond the "banking" approach to power that I spoke of in Chapter 3, where every social maneuver is oriented toward dominance of the classroom discourse, toward a communal or affiliative kind of power where their goal was to break down their separation from the other by using their own foibles as the vehicle. These performances came to represent more than a different kind of bid for notoriety; *they were characterized by a desire to experiment with the point of view of the other.* Boys are made into girls, girls become boys; small forays are made into an unscripted terrain where the "roles" of girls and boys are called into question.

Sharing Time: May 17

Mia has brought in parts of her ballet costume from her dance recital. She launches into a story about the performance, demonstrating how her costume looked by standing up and holding the tutu next to her body. Then she shows a huge red powder puff and a sequined crown and choker, putting on the latter for effect and lavishly powdering her nose with the puff. She describes with great delight the events before, during, and after the performance. During questions and comments, Andrew asks to feel the puff and delicately powders his nose with it, then says, exclaiming in the voice of an elderly dowager, "Oh my, it's loverly." Then he asks, "At recess, can I use this?"

SCRIPTING THE CROSSING

Before I began to explore the children's understandings of gender, a curious event had evolved in my classroom and continued from year to year, primarily because I found it to be transformative for every group of children with whom I worked. For the rest of the world, this event was labeled "Our Class Play," but in reality it was something more.

In April of one year, a class of first graders kept asking me when we were going to "do a play." This took me a bit by surprise because much of what we did involved drama, but obviously the question meant more. It was a request for something different from the small performances that were part of our work in various subject areas, something bigger, more formal, and definitely in front of a large audience "with costumes and stuff." I thought about it, knowing that I was not interested in doing a scripted play with 6-year-olds, but also wondering what other kind of play we might attempt. I came in a few days later with a proposal which the children in that class accepted immediately. My suggestion was that we do a play, but one the children would have to make up. I had only a few requirements: first, it could not have superheroes or cartoon figures as characters, and second, it had to take place "a long time ago."

Those rules were agreeable to the class, and we proceeded with the process, figuring out problems as we encountered them. Early on there was a big concern. Once we had established the setting and a time frame, certain children (by now we can probably describe a profile of them) immediately insisted on deciding who the characters were and which ones they would play, and other children sat mutely by and waited to be told what they would be. (We can probably also guess who *they* were.) I unilaterally added a new rule: to get into the play, you had to "write yourself into the story," and *everybody* had to be in the play or we couldn't have it. The children agonized: what would they (the ones with the ideas) do if the other children wouldn't help or say what they wanted to be? How would the play ever end if we didn't decide at the beginning how and when it was over? How would the characters get "in"? I said I didn't know any of the answers, but that together we would find out.

All these questions were eventually answered, and the answers began with a simple posture. When we came to an impasse, a point at which the story could no longer continue because it needed more action and characters, we waited quietly until some timid child cleared her throat and said she had an idea. She would then "write" herself into our narrative, and other children would ruminate and consult, and soon new ideas would rise up and be agreed upon.

The first year of the play was about a wicked and greedy king who owned everything one could want, and his desire for the ivory teeth and the golden scales of the dragon. The King was played by Mahmoud, a gruff African-American child whose feelings of deprivation and anger about his life had often overwhelmed him with depression throughout the year. Mahmoud knew immediately that he was that king, and he reveled in the idea of owning everything and having power over everyone.

His best knight was named Alvinella, and was played by Alison (who, in the tradition of Mia, Ellen, and Josie, was a risk taker). There were Palace Guards, a kind, timid, fearful Dragon, a tiny Fairy, a Queen, and Princesses, and the play ended with an unusual twist that Mahmoud consented to and enjoyed performing: the King, refusing to leave his precious gold, silver, and jewels to save himself, perished as his palace fell down around him.

The story was written on huge sheets of paper that we hung all around the meeting area, adding pages as we wrote. When it came time for rehearsals, we had a new problem: how would they know what to say? You'll know, I answered, because you know the story. And they did. One child said she wanted to be the "Storyteller" so that everyone would remember the story, and that became her role. Each day we rehearsed the play, figuring out what to say, and orchestrating the children's placements and movements on the stage. Each day the "script" changed, as children rethought their words and added to them. After two weeks in which the play became ever more complex, we made our costumes and sets and performed it. It was hilarious, and filled with metaphors about the life of each child in the classroom. I didn't understand at the time what the children were doing, but when they were finished and had performed it in public, they had changed, both personally and as a class.

Punsters, Jokesters, Beggars, and Lunatics

Subsequent years brought new and daffy stories, and the improvisational format remained the same. The plays took on an existential flavor reminiscent of Beckett's *Waiting for Godot*. Children in the plays parodied themselves, switched genders, revised fairy tales, had long, rambling phenomenological conversations onstage, and delved deeply into their understandings of themselves as public people. For example, I watched a child who was unable all year to communicate effectively with other children because of his obscure use of language and puns create a character who went onstage at different intervals in the play and told very bad jokes to his fellow actors, who then threw him off the stage. He kept coming back with a new bad joke only to be thrown off the stage, until finally he came in with a joke they could understand, and they *really* laughed, and let him stay onstage. He "wrote" that character and designed that sequence but was stumped as to how to end his part. The other children "wrote" the resolution for him, and during rehearsal, when he kept trying to identify a "good" joke to tell, they kept telling him to try again until he got the right one.

IMAGINING NEW WORLDS

To use imagination is to summon up an "as if," to look at things as if they could be otherwise.
                                                                  —*Greene (1995, p. 5)*

The plays now appear to me as the final melding of the children's unofficial social work with the official agenda of the classroom, the development of a kind of "permeable" curriculum (Dyson, 1993). They became an exercise in taking the individual and whole group performances we have seen in earlier chapters, some of which had been evolving for two years, and writing them into a formal script or narrative that represented a collective metaphor for the class as it imagined it might be. And because the plays were meant to be performed in public for their parents, family, and friends, they held up in full view a communal perspective on the world at large. Like all plays, the script embodied the lives of the writers, but it was also about the world they lived in together. It is interesting, I think, to take a look at the kinds of characters the children in this book designed for themselves and the content of their plays from two consecutive years to show how they finally caricatured their relationships with each other and with the world at large.

Year One: The Dungeon

Characters

Donald	*The Lunatic*
Tom	*A Tiny Devil*

Tony	A Sorcerer
Molly	A Dragon
Michael	A Slumbering Ogre
Daniel	A Changeling
Rachel	A Unicorn
Yukiko	A Forest Fairy
Ellen	The Queen
Hiroyasu	The King
Charles	A Hunchback
Josie	A Frog
Eli	A Puppy
Andrew	A Beggar

In this play, a lunatic is sent to the royal dungeon by Queen Ellen because he was "too gross, and talked nonsense all the time." The lunatic, feeling he's been wrongly imprisoned "for just being a bit gross," something he doesn't seem able to control, sends for his friends to help him. Each character subsequently gets stuck in the dungeon, able to get in using whatever skills he or she has, but unable to get out. For example, Tony, the Sorcerer, is called in and his spells continuously backfire throughout the play, causing explosions that do nothing to free anyone, but endanger his friends. Tom, the Tiny Devil, walks in by slipping between the bars, and then spends his time trying to figure out how he could be small enough to get in, but too large to get out. Andrew, the Beggar, wanders on and off stage, unaware of being imprisoned as the cast berates him and throws garbage each time he begs, "Money for the poor. Money for the poor." In the end they relent and give him money, which surprises him so much that he is left speechless. Finally, even the King Hiroyasu ends up in the dungeon because he can't convince the guards that he really is the King.

Throughout the play the characters sit in a line of chairs on the stage with invisible bars, talking to one another about how to get out. Every now and then, one of them makes a halfhearted effort to escape, only to bounce off the bars and return to his or her chair. Eventually, only the Frog, the Dog, and the Changeling, who has been onstage as a tree for the whole time, are still free. The Frog and the Dog persuade the Changeling to help them free their companions. The Changeling turns himself into a key and liberates the prisoners, except for Donald, the Lunatic, who decides he likes the dungeon and refuses to leave.

Year Two: The Dinner Wars

Characters

Charles	*Queen Petunia*
Nathaniel	*The King*
Latia	*Princess Marigold*
Dierdre	*The Court Artist*
Daniel	*A Maid in Waiting*
Alexis	*The Royal Cook*
Mia	*The Narrator*
Michael	*A Shepherd with Five Invisible Sheep*
Eli	*The Archer*
Andrew	*A Scout*
Phillip	*The Spy*
Josie	*A Soldier on a Very Slow Horse*
Rachel	*A Fairy*
Germaine	*Pepper, the Dog*

From the beginning of the writing of this play the children conceptualized it as being "about a silly war over dinner." The play opened with Queen Petunia (Charles) and King Nathaniel sitting down to dinner with Princess Marigold. When the Royal Cook set the dinner on the table, the Queen was delighted.

> "Oh, my favorite," she said, "Chinese food!"
> "Rats," said the King, "I'm sick of Chinese food. We only ever eat Chinese food!"
> "But dear," said Queen Petunia, "Princess Marigold and I just love Chinese food, and that's all we want to eat."
> "Well, I don't," said the King. "I hate your stupid Chinese food and I won't eat it anymore!"
> "Oh yeah, dearie," snarled the Queen. "Then, guess what?" she said, as she took off one shoe, "I declare war on you!" She threw the shoe on the floor with great force.
> "Well, you know what?" returned the King. "I declare war on you, too!" He bent over and started to untie his sneaker, then yanked it off his foot and threw it to the ground. "So there!" he said, and stomped off the stage.

Thus began what the children came to call *The Dinner Wars*. Charles had decided upon beginning rehearsals that he wanted to speak with a brogue, so the class agreed that the plays were set in Ireland. The plot consisted of the two warring camps' preparations for war. Charles dressed for the performance in a red satin dress with a full skirt, petticoats, high heels, red purse, white gloves, and a brown wig. He exuded an air of authority and good breeding. He was constantly trailed by Daniel, his maid, who sported a long dress with apron, gray wig, and high heels, and Latia, Princess Marigold, who was dressed elegantly in a long gown and high heels. She was the essence of haughtiness. King Nathaniel wore sneakers, jeans, and a large crown, and as the play went on, he became more and more comfortable with his role, emerging as a quick, ad-libbing king, a persona that had gradually emerged over the course of the year but took full form in the play.

Each side collected soldiers, and each potential soldier had to "prove" he or she had a useful skill for a war. Eli, the Archer, came equipped with bow and arrows, but designed his part to be that of an unsuccessful archer who simply could not launch his arrows into the air. Phillip was a spy who said nothing, but snuck into the enemy camp without ever being seen. Germaine wanted only to play a dog whose main interest in the war, and in the world, was food. He qualified for the King's side when he admitted that what he really liked to eat was "shrimp, fried in butter and also some garlic." King Nathaniel, whose face took on an ecstatic look at the thought of such a meal, immediately recruited Pepper for his side, exclaiming, "At least you know good food when you see it!"

When the armies were assembled for battle, they were completely unable to fight because they kept forgetting who was on their side and who was the enemy. As a result, Queen Petunia challenged King Nathaniel to a duel. The children had decided that the dual should be a fencing match. Since the girls didn't think the queen should use a sword, Charles, who had been quite disappointed with that decision, suggested they use fake fences for weapons as an amusing twist to the action, explaining the play on words to the rest of the class with a great deal of help and assistance from Michael, the wordmaster.

The duel was quite dramatic, with a great deal of grunting and hurling of insults. At one point Queen Petunia called a time-out to powder her nose. The King sat down to rest as Petunia pulled powder puff and mirror out of her pocketbook and spent quite a bit of time fixing her face. "There, dearie," she said, when she was done, "Time in!" and the duel resumed. Finally the duel was ended when both parties decided they were too hungry to continue fighting. A brief reconciliation followed, and once again the royal couple sat down to dinner as they had in the beginning. The Royal Cook brought dinner in, and this time the King was happy.

"Pizza!" he shouted. "My favorite!"

"I hate pizza!" said the Queen. "Give me anything else: sushi, fried rice, bagels, tacos, anything but pizza!"

"Oh yeah? Well I want pizza!" returned the King.

"Oh yeah, dearie? Well then, I declare war on you!" said Queen Petunia, as she threw her shoe on the floor.

"Well, I declare war on you, too!" shouted the King, as he struggled to untie his sneaker yet again and throw it onto the floor.

Mia, the narrator, had had enough. "That's it!" she yelled, storming onto the center of the stage. "I'm getting really tired of this, and I refuse to let this stupid war go on any longer. The story is over!" She slammed her script shut, and the cast fell down, ending the play.

CREATING INTERTEXTS

Social processes . . . involve crossing boundaries and intermingling texts in ways that bring together official and unofficial worlds . . . yield an intertext . . . a reverberation of connections.

—Dyson (1993, p. 108)

In each of the plays, the children created "intertexts," symbolic worlds in which their personae were magnified so as to highlight both how they were perceived by others in the day-to-day transactions of the classroom and their own reflections on those perceptions. Each character seemed to embody this double vision, one that reflected both his or her own role in creating the persona and the role of the other in maintaining it. The subtexts that had reverberated through both classes of children also gained symbolic form in the plays, becoming visible in the words and the actions of the children. Because the plays were always co-constructed, they represented a collective understanding of the subtexts, an acknowledgment and a representation, as it were, of what the children had been playing out for two years, both as audience and as actors.

For example, Tony, as the Sorcerer in the first play, was one of the first characters to be called to the dungeon by the Lunatic, because he was thought to be unquestionably the most powerful individual in the kingdom. But the Sorcerer was never able to remember how to cast his spells correctly, and eventually, when he resorted to brute strength, he was unable to break through the invisible bars. Rachel, the Unicorn, questioned the power of the Sorcerer who threatened her with a spell, whereupon she elegantly speared him with her horn, leaving him humbled. And Donald, the Lunatic, reveled in his role as the character whose desire to be free gathered a large coterie of would-be saviors around him, only to realize in the end that he enjoyed the solitude, safety, and peacefulness of living alone in the dungeon.

In the second play, Charles, both feminine and gruff as Queen Petunia, played with the meaning of male and female, interweaving both aspects into his character's words and actions. Eli, as the ineffectual Archer, highlighted his inability to become what he desired, muttering as each arrow fell to the floor in front of him, "I'll never get this right . . . maybe the next time." Rachel, the Fairy, had the most powerful magic as she, with very few words, temporarily turned the King into an ant after he had accidentally trampled her flower home. Germaine, as Pepper the Dog, stayed on the outskirts of the battle action, watching, nipping at the heels of his fellow soldiers, but staying clear of hand-to-hand combat. Dierdre, the official Court Artist, spent the entire play standing in front of an easel at center stage, sketching, painting, and observing, but never joining in the action or dialogue—with one exception, when she stopped the action in mid-battle by a few quiet words, and then pointed wordlessly to the picture on the easel. At that moment the battle ceased, and the actors (and the audience) applauded appreciatively for a few seconds before the battle resumed.

It was clear to me as the plays unfolded each year that they embodied a collective movement in which the class recapitulated and reconciled their many performances and personae with their desires to be seen, finally, as co-actors for whom daily life was a brave experimentation with new ways of being. As their teacher, I could observe how the final performance cemented relationships and loosened hierarchies. I could also see how hard the children had worked, sometimes without my awareness, at knowing each other, at recognizing their respective struggles to be understood and to gain respect from others, at confronting their limitations, and at creating new social and moral landscapes.

THE DISCOURSE OF LIVED CULTURES

The discourse of lived cultures . . . needs to interrogate how people create stories, memories, and narratives that posit a sense of determination and agency . . . the conscious and unconscious material through which members of dominant and subordinate groups offer accounts of who they are and present different readings of the world.

—Giroux (1985, p. 39)

It is clear to me now, as I finish writing this book, that teaching (and for me, by extension, teacher research) is always an unfinished project. The "worlds of possibility" that I spoke of earlier and hoped to create for children have changed. When I was younger I thought I could orchestrate those worlds through my understanding of what *ought* to be.

Now I understand that I cannot orchestrate what ought to be when I do not understand what *is*. And further, I know that what is changes with each new class of children I teach, and with each additional year of life that I myself experience. Who I am, as Paulo Freire points out (Freire & Macedo, 1987), is something I can apprehend only within the context of social relations. And I would add that who I am, or who an individual child I teach is and will become, is always a continuing piece of work, constructed in relation to the other, in conversation with the other, and, in the best of all possible worlds, in communion with the other.

Within this dialogic framework, schooling becomes a moving form and requires teachers to scrutinize constantly the moment they are living in, the assumptions they are acting upon, the convictions they hold close. Within this dialogic framework, one that has evolved for me over the course of researching and writing this book, I have learned something that is both disturbing and exhilarating: this book, like all social artifacts, is both true and not true. In it I have described a world I lived and participated in, but that world was a limited and particular one, and the "moves" each of us made in building our social identities and awarenesses can never be replicated. But within this story is a lesson that speaks to the dynamic and evolutionary nature of a classroom community. The laboratory that the classroom represents is one in which all children *and their teachers* can develop new understandings of who they are and who they aspire to be. It is a place where teachers can scrutinize their own standards and beliefs, can doubt what they thought they knew, and can acknowledge the power of the prosaic world and celebrate the transformations that the poetic world allows. Teachers and the children placed in their care are mutually engaged in this endeavor. Each new class presents a new world of possibility, new forms to study, and new potential for building powerful communities of belonging.

Afterword

The fundamental point is an understanding of social life as something not given in advance and a priori, but as having an ineradicable aspect of being constituted by its participants in an ongoing, evolving way. Those who accept this point can agree on giving priority to discovery of what is actually done in local settings and of what it means to its participants. The concomitant of that priority is an empowering of participants as sources of knowledge.

—Hymes (1980, p. xiv)

Let us celebrate the uniqueness of each class of children, and every child in it! Just when I thought *I* had understood what gender might mean in a classroom community, in walked Sophia, Barbara, and Jamilla. And what I thought I knew was turned once more on its head.

The purpose of this afterword is to extend further the thinking and reflections of my readers. I hope it will emphasize the complexity of classroom life and illuminate what the process of teacher research might add to discussions of charged issues such as gender and race. I also want my readers to have their conclusions about these issues jumbled around, just as my conclusions were jumbled. (I choose the word "jumbled" here to emphasize the nature of the disruption: it wasn't a contradiction in clear terms, or a reversal, but rather a toppling of my sense of continuity.) I hope to leave the reader with a further reflection on the process of classroom research, and how each new research experience refines our understanding of what this unique process might mean for children, for teachers, and for the integrity of their actions as a community.

BEGINNING AGAIN WITH A NEW CLASS

In September of the year following my leave, I returned to teaching first grade with a new class of 6-year-olds. It became evident early on that there was something quite different about the chemistry of this group. As the year progressed I knew that this class also had a great deal to teach me about the issues of the subtextual, of power, and of performance. Most notable was the emergence of a powerful group of girls, who, separately and together, had a very obvious social agenda: They wanted to be in charge of the social discourse of the class, and, like the bad boys from earlier classes, they worked hard to consolidate their power and maintain it through the use of stories and public performances.

This chapter presents just a few representative excerpts from audiotapes of sharing time focusing on the words of a few children to point out how much each group of children and each child in that group has to teach us about the questions in this book and many others. As I worked with these children, I found myself once again questioning assumptions I had made about boys and girls and the understandings they bring to school. What was not called into question, however, was the power of performance as a vehicle for developing both individual and communal understandings of possible worlds. Although the girls orchestrated the power plays, each of us savored the dramas and participated in them wholeheartedly. And over time we became intoxicated by their notion that anything was possible *for anyone*.

A consistent storytelling theme was that the girls had daring and mischievous adventures that often included other members who the girls would have to save.

Sharing Time: March 14

Sophia begins by rubbing her hands together as she smiles and slowly surveys the audience.

SOPHIA: Once upon a time, there was a little girl named Sophia, and she called all of her friends. She called: (Sophia names every girl in the audience.)

JAMILLA: No boys!

SOPHIA: And then I called all of the little boys to come and play with me. (The boys cheer.) I called: (She names all of the boys in the class.) All the little boys were there, and Joey went swimming. We were going to meet him there. Then we had a little party and we ran into the middle of the street. And the cars were going 'Vroom, Vroom, Vroom!', and then I went out and put a little stop sign so the children could cross the street. We went to the beach and I jumped into the water, and it was so hot! And I got Ed a sea star . . .

There was a little man there, who started walking down the beach. And all of the sudden the little man fell! He was so teeny, that teeny little man, that he fell into the sand and drownded! In the sand! And then I stepped on him! Then I picked him up by the foot, and threw him in the water. He said, "Help!" Then Barbara picked him up. She found a clam that was closed. She opened it up, and there wasn't anything inside, so she put the little man in, and threw him out to sea. Then the little man's wife and family came. And there were 13 of them! So we found 13 clams, and guess what we did then?

ALL: What?

SOPHIA: We put all of 'em in a shell, and threw them out to sea with the little man!

EQUAL LAND

Sharing Time: March 15

JAMILLA: There was a land. It was always Equal Land. There were three boys and three girls. If the boys had egg salad, the girls had egg salad. The children didn't like it there so they left and went to a new land. They got new parents. But they didn't like their parents, so they sent away to Florida for new parents. And they got one called Big Mamma, and a father, Little Joe. Two children got sent away: the prettiest girl and the best boy. Jamilla and Joey. But they weren't in love. No. Not in love. They were a great *team.*

The three girls were very powerful in an unusual way. They had tremendous influence over the stories told in the class—not over genre or style, but over content. Stories had to be adventurous and exciting, and they were to include everyone, but a person's stories were controlled *only* by that person. The class could not dictate to them or to anyone else what was or wasn't a fair storyline, or whether someone was or wasn't in the story. This consistently placed a factor of uncertainty and surprise in all of their sharing time stories, and in their interpersonal relationships. They were extremely creative and also unpredictable, so that very few of us could guess what they would or wouldn't do next.

For the same reasons, I found them quite difficult to control. There was an air of chaos they created when I was teaching. It was not the air of direct challenge to my authority that I had experienced with bad boys in the past, but was rather mischevousness. For example, it was not unusual for Sophia, who sat right up front by the teacher as a rule, to very slyly pull a prank while my intern or I were teaching. On more than one occasion, I finished a lesson only to look down and see that Sophia had tied my shoelaces together. It was funny, I had to admit, but extremely undignified, and on its own level it represented a very direct challenge to my authority. I was definitely learning something new about power.

Sharing Time: March 28

Sophia is sharing a picture from her art journal:

SOPHIA: This is the public gardens where the swan boats are. This is the daddy and the mommy and their baby. These clouds are made out of bunny rabbits. And . . . me and Barbara are on the other side. And the duckies see our bread, and we're going to go feed them. And the sun is smiling because he sees another piece of the sun that's not really sun. And he sees the reflection in the water, and he goes to get the sun in the water. And then he comes out and he's steaming! And he goes day to night. Questions or comments.

VICTOR: Which one's the daddy?

SOPHIA: Can't you tell? The mommies do not get pretty feathers. He's the daddy. 'Cause those feathers are for hiding in the grass.

JAMILLA: Did you say there were bunnies?

SOPHIA: Here (points to the top of the picture)! It's Violet and her husband. In heaven.

[By this time, Violet, our pet bunny, had passed away.]

   Violet got married. Her husband's at work. Violet went up in the clouds and put them together into a funny rabbit.

ALLEN: Why did you draw Violet in the clouds?

SOPHIA: Because it's *my* journal, and I can draw whatever I want!

   If I want to draw you in a plane, I can.

   If I want you swimming in the water, I can.

   If I want you in a car, I can.

   If I want to draw Violet, I can!

Sophia's words underscored the intensity with which she tried to control the dynamics of her performances and her educational process. She and Jamilla were both reluctant readers, although Barbara learned to read appropriately for a first grader. All the girls spent most of their time and energy orchestrating their social interactions both in and outside the classroom, and everything was an occasion for a performance of sorts, whether it was mayhem in the blocks, or grossing out the boys at a child's birthday party when they rubbed ice cream all over their faces, rather than licking the ice cream off the cone in the proper way. Ironically, it was always the boys who complained about their misbehavior, finding it to be, I think, impressive but shocking.

Their orchestrations, however, often spilled over into the public sphere of sharing time. Like the powerful girls we met earlier in this book, they did not like to manipulate other children behind the scenes, but fair play was very important to them. But fair play didn't mean just equity; it meant self-determination and in some sense *enforcing* standards of behavior.

Sharing Time: March 22

Jamilla tells a very naughty story in which she kills off Ed and then Billy. As the story progresses, Sophia keeps saying, "Kill me! Kill me!"

WILL: Why did you make it so violent?
JAMILLA: 'Cause I wanted to.
ALLEN: But you hurt their feelings.
JAMILLA: The reason I do it is because Ed teases people, and also when I ask Billy for things, he hits me. And sometimes he says these words to me, and I hate them. And (to Billy), you don't know that I do.
ED: I'm gonna get you.
JAMILLA: You, you guys make these things happen, Ed. You know you tease people. And Billy, he gets his anger up.
BILLY: Yeah, but I been learning to control that.

CROSSING OVER

Clearly these girls had been crossing over the imaginary boundary between the sexes for months. They were intensely involved in many different kinds of imaginative experiences. They outgrossed the boys, waxed poetic about high heels and jewels, built elaborate social networks, and created mayhem in the blocks-and-art corner. It was not unusual to find Sophia and Barbara covered head to toe with tempera paint as a result of a contest to see who could splatter the most paint on their paper, or for Jamilla to be masterminding an elaborate "candy store" that sold our classroom Legos to any taker for real pennies. At the same time all of them brought different petite stuffed animals to play with at recess: they made the bunnies little burrows, but in the mud, of course; cooked them meals of grass and flowers; and then hung them up by their toes from bushes for misbehaving.

Personally I was confused as to what, if anything, I ought to do about the shenanigans of the three girls. Unlike the bad boys I had observed, they were operating in ways that did not intimidate other children. When it came to learning, with the exception of my shoelaces being tied together, their behavior was not a disruptive influence. Or was it? I really had a hard time coming to a conclusion. Meanwhile, the other girls in the class were carrying on more traditional, low-profile roles, but they took obvious pleasure in the daring and the notoriety of their friends. The boys were also maintaining fairly traditional first-grade profiles, although they regularly steeled themselves (with barely concealed glee) for some new prank or story. I guess, overall, there was simply a carnival atmosphere in the classroom at all times.

PERISHABLE ART

The classroom is like perishable art. It has an evanescence that makes it, for me at least, energizing and joyful, but also bittersweet, because the events are impossible to hold in time as a complete entity. Being a teacher researcher, however, has given me some capacity to grab onto fragments of the life that is streaming by me. But I have found that I am not able to function in that process as a dispassionate observer. I am a full member of a unique culture. I am an aboriginal. Sophia, Barbara, Jamilla, and I are all originals in our classroom, and the classroom itself is an original, a contained sociogeographical region. It has its own topography, its own language, stories, rituals, memories, incantations, and governance structure. And as this research has shown, each new class I teach becomes a new tribe with new fauna and flora and a new topography to be mapped.

Thus, to my mind, when a teacher considers what it means to truly inspect the cultural and political boundaries of the classroom through the research process, there are two notions that must be held constant: first, each classroom is a unique, living community; and second, each individual within that community represents an evolving consciousness. In other words, the research setting is indeterminate, unpredictable, or, as Bakhtin says (in Morson & Emerson, 1990) "unfinalizable." Nothing that has happened before can be expected to happen again in the same way, and everything that has happened before is absorbed into the body of classroom life.

So after four years of classroom research in which I had to continually throw over what I thought I had known about gender, in walks Sophia, who, with the help of her friends, lays down a new layer of complexity to the subject. In effect, Sophia enters and claims territory for herself. She prevents me from making the issue of what it means to be a girl in a primary classroom in any way static. She throws in my face what I thought I had known about girls in public. She reclaims the territory of her social world as unique aboriginal territory, and my place as a tribal member alters once again as I am forced to consider how our lives and our awareness of the world do and don't match.

Sharing Time: May 2

SOPHIA: Once upon a time in a far, far town in a far, far city, there lived a mommy and a daddy, and another mommy and daddy. And they had babies: Sophia and Barbara. And so they grew up. And they became handy around the house. And they washed the dishes, helped push Daddy out of bed, and got him to work, cleaned the yard . . . but one day they decided to run away. They got a boat and set sail down a river. They saw a Violet in the river. "Stop the boat!" said Sophia.

They stopped and jumped into the river and followed the Violet to a secret hole. And the one Violet led them to a secret place. There was a mountain of Violets! A volcano of Violets! Sophia threw a rock into the volcano. The volcano erupted! And Violets came out of the volcano! They could only choose one. Every Violet put on the cutest face, so they had to take all the Violets.

References

Abrahams, R. D. (1976). *Talking black*. Rowley, MA: Newbury House.

American Association of University Women Educational Foundation and the Wellesley College Center for Research on Women (1993). *How schools shortchange girls*. Washington, DC: AAUW Educational Foundation.

Ashton-Warner, S. (1958). *Spinster*. New York: Simon and Schuster.

Ashton-Warner, S. (1963). *Teacher*. New York: Simon and Schuster.

Atwell, N. (1986). *In the middle: Writing, reading, and learning with adolescents*. Portsmouth, NH: Boynton/Cook.

Bauman, R. (1977). *Verbal art as performance*, Rowley, MA: Newbury House.

Bakhtin, M. M. (1981). *The dialogic imagination*. Austin, TX: University of Texas Press.

Bakhtin, M. M. (1984). *Problems of Dostoevsky's poetics*. (Caryl Emerson, Ed. & Trans.). Minneapolis, MN: University of Minnesota Press.

Bakhtin, M. M. (1986). *Speech genres and other late essays*. Austin, TX: University of Texas Press.

Becker, A. L. (1992). Silences across languages: An essay. In C. Kramsch & S. McConnell-Genet (Eds.), *Text and context: Cross-disciplinary perspectives on language study* (pp. 115–123). Lexington, MA: Heath.

Best, R. (1983). *We've all got scars: What boys and girls learn in elementary school*. Bloomington, IN: Indiana University Press.

Cobb, E. (1994). *The ecology of imagination in early childhood*. Dallas: Spring.

Cochran-Smith, M. (1991). Learning to teach against the grain. *Harvard Educational Review, 61*(3), 279–310.

Dyson, A. (1993). *Social worlds of children learning to write in an urban primary school*. New York: Teachers College Press.

Edwards, D., & Mercer, N. (1987). *Common knowledge: The development of understanding in the classroom*. London: Methuen.

Estrada, K., & McClaren, P. (1993). A dialogue on multiculturalism in democratic culture. *Educational Researcher, 22*(3), 27–33.

Freire, P., & Macedo, D. (1987). *Literacy: Reading the word and the world*. New York: Bergin and Garvey.

Frye, N. (1964). *The educated imagination*. Bloomington: University of Indiana Press.

Gallas, K. (1994). *The languages of learning: How children talk, write, dance, draw, and sing their understanding of the world.* New York: Teachers College Press.

Gallas, K. (1995). *Talking their way into science: Hearing children's questions and theories, responding with curricula.* New York: Teachers College Press.

Geertz, C. (1973). *The interpretation of cultures: Selected essays.* New York: Basic Books.

Giroux, H. (1985). Critical pedagogy, cultural politics, and the discourse of experience. *Journal of Education,* 167(2), 22–41.

Greene, M. (1995, Fall). Metaphor and possibility. *On Common Ground,* 5, 5–21.

Grumet, M. (1988). *Bitter milk.* Amherst, MA: University of Massachusetts.

Heath, S. B. (1983). *Ways with words: Language, life, and work in communities and classrooms.* Cambridge, UK: Cambridge University Press.

Hymes, D. (1980). Language in education: Ethnolinguistic essays. Washington, DC: Center for Applied Linguistics.

Lewis, M., & Simon, R. (1986). A Discourse Not Intended for Her: Learning and Teaching Within Patriarchy. *Harvard Educational Review,* 56(4), 457–472.

Merleau-Ponty, M. (1964). *Phenomenology of perception.* New York: Humanities Press.

Morson, G. S., & Emerson, C. (1990). *Mikhail Bakhtin: Creation of a prosaics.* Stanford: Stanford University Press.

Opie, I. A., & Opie, P. (1959). *The lore and language of school children.* Oxford: University Press.

Ortega y Gassett, J. (1957). *Man and people.* New York: Norton.

Paley, V. (1984). *Boys and girls: Superheroes in the doll corner.* Chicago: University of Chicago Press.

Potter, B. (1909). *The Tale of the Flopsy bunnies.* New York: Warne.

Smitherman, G. (1986). *Talkin' and testifyin': The language of black America.* Detroit: Wayne State University Press.

Tannen, D. (1990). *You just don't understand: Women and men in conversation.* New York: Ballantine Press Books.

Thorne, B. (1993). *Gender play: Girls and boys in school.* New Brunswick, NJ: Rutgers University Press.

West, C., & Zimmerman, D. H. (1987). Doing gender. *Gender & Society* 1, 125–151.

Williams, P. (1991). *The alchemy of race and rights.* Cambridge, MA: Harvard University Press.

Index

About the Author

Karen Gallas is an elementary teacher in Brookline, Massachusetts, and is also a member of the Brookline Teacher Research Seminar. She has taught children in the public schools of Massachusetts since 1972, with the exception of the four years when she was a member of the faculty at the University of Maine (1981–1985). She received her doctorate in education from Boston University in 1981. Her work as a teacher researcher has focused on the role of the arts in teaching and learning, on children's language in the classroom, and on the process of teacher research. She has published two books, *The Languages of Learning: How Children Talk, Write, Dance, Draw, and Sing Their Understanding of the World*, and *Talking Their Way Into Science: Hearing Children's Questions and Theories, Responding With Curricula*, both published by Teachers College Press.